EX LIBRIS

DANNIE
ABSE

ASK THE
MOON

NEW AND COLLECTED POEMS
1948-2014

HUTCHINSON
LONDON

Published by Hutchinson 2014

2 4 6 8 10 9 7 5 3 1

Copyright © Dannie Abse 2014

Dannie Abse has asserted his right under the Copyright, Designs and
Patents Act 1988 to be identified as the author of this work.

First published in Great Britain in 2014 by
Hutchinson
Random House, 20 Vauxhall Bridge Road,
London SW1V 2SA

www.randomhouse.co.uk

Addresses for companies within The Random House Group Limited can be
found at: www.randomhouse.co.uk/offices.htm

The Random House Group Limited Reg. No. 954009

A CIP catalogue record for this book
is available from the British Library

ISBN 9780091958916

The Random House Group Limited supports the Forest Stewardship
Council® (FSC®), the leading international forest-certification organisation.
Our books carrying the FSC label are printed on FSC®-certified paper.
FSC is the only forest-certification scheme supported by the leading
environmental organisations, including Greenpeace. Our paper procurement
policy can be found at www.randomhouse.co.uk/environment

Typeset by Palimpsest Book Production Ltd, Falkirk, Stirlingshire

Printed and bound in Great Britain by CPI Group (UK) Ltd, Croydon, CR0 4YY

Acknowledgements

Over many decades I have accumulated many debts to those who have engaged sympathetically with my work, not least my editor at Hutchinson, Tony Whittome. I thank him and the others including my agent and friend Robert Kirby and Sian Williams. I'm also particularly grateful to Lynne Hjelmgaard for her invaluable help in the preparation of this book. *Ask the Moon* is dedicated once again to my late wife, Joan, whose earlier encouragement was always discriminating and vital; to whom I once wrote,

'Love, read this though it has little meaning
For by reading this you give me meaning.'

D. A.

Author's Note

When I reread these *Collected Poems* I realise how much they are rooted in and from my life experiences, some mundane, some dramatic. I recall words of Rilke whom I read when I was a young medical student, 'In order to write a single verse one must be able to return in thought to unexpected encounters, to days of childhood that are still indistinct, to nights of love . . . But one must also have been beside the dying, must have sat beside the dead in a room with open windows and fitful noises.'

I have experienced such things as so many others have, and I have done my best to tell of them in the best way I can, with what gifts I have. I hope these poems are universal enough to give others mental and heartfelt pleasure, in their comedy and in their grief.

Dannie Abse, September 2014

Proposal

Herschel, thrilled, observed a new star
and named it to honour a King;

Dr Livingstone found for his Queen
a waterfall, 'smoke which sounded';

and tactful Corot gave Daumier
a house 'to upset the landlord'.

What dare I promise? Mountain signposts
are few and treasures I have none.

Yet come with me, congenial, far,
up the higher indigo roads.

There, memory is imagination
and we may find an eagle's feather.

Contents

Contents

A Small Desperation 1961–1967

Funland and Other Poems 1967–1972

On the Evening Road 1989-1994

Arcadia, One Mile 1994-1998

New Poems, 1998-2002

Running Late 2002-2005

Two for Joy 2005–2010

Revisions and New 2013-2014

The Uninvited

They came into our lives unasked for.
There was light momentarily, a flicker of wings,
a dance, a voice, and then they went out
again, like a light, leaving us not so much
in darkness, but in a different place
and alone as never before.

So we have been changed
and our vision no longer what it was,
and our hopes no longer what they were;
so a piece of us has gone out with them also,
a cold dream subtracted without malice,

the weight of another world added also,
and we did not ask, we did not ask ever
for those who stood smiling
and with flowers before the open door.

We did not beckon them in, they came in uninvited,
the sunset pouring from their shoulders,
so they walked through us as they would through water,
and we are here, in a different place,
changed and incredibly alone,
and we did not know, we do not know ever.

Epithalamion

Singing, today I married my white girl
beautiful in a barley field.
Green on thy finger a grass blade curled,
so with this ring I thee wed, I thee wed,
and send our love to the loveless world
of all the living and all the dead.

Now, no more than vulnerable human,
we, more than one, less than two,
are nearly ourselves in a barley field –
and only love is the rent that's due
though the bailiffs of time return anew
to all the living but not the dead.

Shipwrecked, the sun sinks down harbours
of a sky, unloads its liquid cargoes
of marigolds, and I and my white girl
lie still in the barley – who else wishes
to speak, what more can be said
by all the living against the dead?

Come then all you wedding guests:
green ghost of trees, gold of barley,
you blackbird priests in the field,
you wind that shakes the pansy head
fluttering on a stalk like a butterfly;
come the living and come the dead.

Listen flowers, birds, winds, worlds,
tell all today that I married
more than a white girl in the barley –

for today I took to my human bed
flower and bird and wind and world,
and all the living and all the dead.

Song for Dov Shamir

Working is another way of praying.
You plant in Israel the soul of a tree.
You plant in the desert the spirit of gardens.

Praying is another way of singing.
You plant in the tree the soul of lemons.
You plant in the gardens the spirit of roses.

Singing is another way of loving.
You plant in the lemons the spirit of your son.
You plant in the roses the soul of your daughter.

Loving is another way of living.
You plant in your daughter the spirit of Israel.
You plant in your son the soul of the desert.

1948

Soho: Saturday Night

Always Cain, anonymous amidst the poor,
Abel dead in his eye, and over his damned sore
a khaki muffler, loiters, a fugitive in Soho,
enters The Golden Calf Club and hears Esau,

dishevelled and drunk, cursing kith and kin.
'A mess of pottage!' Esau strokes an unshaven chin
and strikes a marble table-top. Then hairy hands
fidget dolefully, raise up a glass of gin.

Outside, Joseph, dyspnoeic, regards a star
convexing over Dean Street, coughs up a flower
from ruined lungs — rosy petals on his tongue —
recalls the Pit and wounds of many a colour.

Traffic lights change. With tapping white stick
a giant crosses the road between the frantic
taxis. A philistine pimp laughs. Dancing
in The Nude Show Delilah suddenly feels sick.

Ruth, too, the innocent, was gullibly led,
lay down half-clothed on a brassy railing bed
of Mr Boaz of Bayswater. Now, too late, weeps
antiseptic tears, wishes she were dead.

Who goes home? Nebuchadnezzar to the
doss-house where, all night, he'll turn and toss.
Lunchtime, in Soho Square, he munched the grass
and now he howls at strangers as they pass.

In Café Babylon, Daniel, interpreter of dreams,
listens to Belshazzar, a shy lad in his teens:
'A soiled finger moved across the lavatory wall.'
Growing up is not so easy as it seems.

Prophets, like tipsters, awaiting the Advent.
Beggar Job, under the flashing advertisement
for toothpaste, the spirochaete in his brain,
groans. Chalks a lurid picture on the pavement.

The Golden Calf closes. Who goes home? All
tourists to Nod; psalmists from their pub crawl;
they leave unshaved Soho to its dawn furnace
of affliction, its wormwood and its gall.

Letter to Alex Comfort

Alex, perhaps a colour of which neither of us had dreamt
may appear in the test-tube with God knows what admonition.
Ehrlich, certainly, was one who broke down the mental doors,
yet only after his six hundred and sixth attempt.

Koch also, painfully, and with true German thoroughness,
eliminated the impossible to prove that too many of us
are dying from the same disease. Visible, on the slide
at last – Death – and the thin bacilli of an ancient distress.

Still I, myself, don't like Germans, but prefer the unkempt
voyagers who, like butterflies drunk with suns,
can only totter crookedly in the dazed air
to reach, charmingly, their destination as if by accident.

That Greek one, then, is my hero who watched the bath water
rise above his navel, and rushed out naked, 'I found it,
I found it' into the street in all his shining and forgot
that others would only stare at his genitals.
      What laughter!

Or Newton, leaning in Woolsthorpe against the garden wall,
forgot his indigestion and all such trivialities,
but gaped up at heaven in just surprise, and, with
true gravity, witnessed the vertical apple fall.

O what a marvellous observation! Who would have reckoned
that such a pedestrian miracle could alter history,
that, henceforward, everyone must fall, whatever
their rank, at thirty-two feet per second, per second?

You too, I know, have waited for doors to fly open, played
with your cold chemicals, written long letters
to the Press; listened to the truth afraid, and dug deep
into the wriggling earth for a rainbow with an honest spade.

But nothing rises. Neither spectres, nor oil, nor love.
And the old professor must think you mad, Alex, as you rehearse
poems in the laboratory like vows, and curse those clever scientists
who dissect away the wings and haggard heart from the dove.

Leaving Cardiff

I wait in the evening air.
Sea-birds drop down to the sea.
I prepare to sail from where
the docks' derelictions are.

I stand on the deck and stare,
slack hammocks of waves below,
while black shapes upon the pier
make the furthest star seem near.

Now the funnel's negations blow
and my eyes, like spaces, fill,
and the knots of water flow,
pump to my eyes and spill.

For what *who* would choose to go
when *who* sailing made no choice?
Not for one second, I know,
can I be the same man twice.

The straw-coloured flames flare still,
spokes over the long horizon,
and the boats under the hill
of Penarth, unload and move on.

Letter to *The Times*

Sir, I have various complaints to make.
The roses, first. When they are ripped
from the earth expiring, we sigh for them,
prescribe tap-water, aspirin, and salt.
But when we lie down under the same earth,
in a dry silly box, do they revive us?
Their odour of rose-ghosts does not change
at all, and they continue to call out
in their red and white morse the old, old
messages as if nothing had happened. Again,
consider trees. My God, the impresario
trees. Just try, Sir, just try to cut one down
in Fitzjohn's Avenue at three o'clock
in the ordinary afternoon. You will be
prosecuted. Soon the Householders will arrange
themselves into a deranged *mob*. They'll grow
Hitler moustaches, Mussolini chins. Frightful,
and write oathy letters to the Council,
naming you *tree-criminal*. Yet tell me, when
the bombs met their shadows in London,
amidst the ruins of voices, did one tree, just one
tree write an angry note in its sly green ink?
No, they only dropped faded tears in autumn
selfishly thinking of their own hamadryads . . .
BUSINESS AS USUAL was, and is, their trite
slogan. Away then with trees and roses.
They are inhuman. Away also with rivers:
the disgusting Ganges bleeding from Brahma's
big toe; the Rubicon cause of a Civil War;
the Acheron, River of Sorrows; Tiber that drowned
Horatius the One-Eyed; the sweating Rhône,

Rhine, Don, and the vulgar Volga, not to
mention the garrulous Mississippi with its
blatant river-smell. Even the English
rivers can do no more than reflect inverted
values, turn chaste swans upside down
like so many flies on the roof of the waters.
Swans, however, *cannot* swim upside down.
At least, I have never seen them. Is this distortion
of truth deliberate? Has ever one river,
one river, Sir, written eulogies of waterfalls
to plead for the reprieve of Mankind? And stars,
so indifferent and delinquent, stars which we have
decorated with glittering adjectives more numerous
than those bestowed on Helen's eyes − do they
warn us when they fall? Not a hint.
Not a star-wink. They are even too lazy
to shine when we are most awake. Creatures
of night, they are probably up to immoral
purposes. You can't trust a star, that's sure.
So when the greenfly is in the rose,
and the dragonfly drops its shadow in the river;
when the axe hides in the tree with its listening
shriek, and clouds gag the starlight
with grey handkerchiefs − I contend, Sir,
that we should pity them no more,
but concern ourselves with more natural things.

1949

9

Duality

Twice upon a time,
there was a man who had two faces,
two faces but one profile:
not Jekyll and Hyde, not good and bad,
but if one were cut, the other would bleed –
two faces different as hot and cold.

At night, hung on the hooks on the wall
above that man's minatory head,
one wants brass where one wants gold,
one sees white and one sees black,
and one mouth eats the other
until the second sweet mouth bites back.

They dream their separate dreams
hanging on the wall above the bed.
The first voice cries: 'He's not what he seems,'
but the second one sighs: 'He is what he is,'
then one shouts 'wine' and the other screams 'bread',
and so they will all his raving days
until they die on his double-crossed head.

At signposts he must wear them both.
Each would go their separate ways
as the East or the West wind blows –
and dark and light they both would praise,
but one would melt, the other one freeze.

I am that man twice upon this time:
my two voices sing to make one rhyme.
Death I love and Death I hate,

(I'll be with you soon and late).
Love I love and Love I loathe
God I mock and God I prove,
yes, myself I kill, myself I save.

Now, now, I hang these masks on the wall.
Oh Time, take one and leave me all
lest four tears from two eyes fall.

The Trial

The heads around the table disagree,
some say hang him from the gallows tree.

Some say high and some say low
to swing, swing, swing, when the free winds blow.

I wanted to be myself, no more,
so I screwed off the face that I always wore,

I pulled out the nails one by one –
I'd have given that face to anyone.

For those vile features were hardly mine;
to wear another's face is a spiritual crime.

Why, imagine the night when I would wed
to kiss with wrong lips in the bridal bed . . .

But now the crowd screams loud in mockery:
Oh string him up from the gallows tree.

Silence! the Judge commands, or I'll clear the court,
to hang a man up is not a sport –

though some say high and some say low
to swing, swing, swing, when the free winds blow.

Prisoner, allow me once more to ask:
what did you do with your own pure mask?

I told you, your honour, I threw it away,
it was only made of skin-coloured clay.

A face is a man, a bald juryman cries,
for one face lost, another man dies.

Gentlemen, this citizen we daren't acquit
until we know what he did with it.

It was only a face, your honour, that I lost;
how much can such a sad thing cost?

A mask is a lifetime, my bad man,
to replace such a gift nobody can.

Consider the case of that jovial swan
who took a god's face off to put a bird's face on

and Leda swooning by the side of the sea
and the swan's eyes closed in lechery.

No! No! your honour, my aim was just –
I did what every true man must.

Quiet, prisoner! Why I remember a priest remark
that he picked up a dog's face in the dark,

then he got as drunk as a man can be
and barked at God in blasphemy.

But it was a human face, sir, I cast away;
for that offence do I have to pay?

The heads around the table disagree,
some say hang him from the gallows tree.

Some say high and some say low
to swing, swing, swing, when the free winds blow.

At the back of the courtroom quietly stand
his father and mother hand-in-hand.

They can't understand the point of this case
or why he discarded his own dear face.

But it's not *my* face, father, he had said,
I don't want to die in a strange, wrong bed.

Look in the mirror, mother, stare in deep;
is that mask your own, yours to keep?

The mirror is oblong, the clock is round,
all our wax faces go underground.

Once, I built a bridge right into myself
to ransack my soul for invisible wealth

and, afterwards, I tore off my mask because
I found not the person I thought I was.

With the wrong mask, another man's life I live –
I must seek my own face, find my own grave.

The heads around the table disagree,
some say hang him from the gallows tree.

Some say high and some say low
to swing, swing, swing, when the free winds blow.

I'll sum up, the severe Judge moans,
showing the white of his knucklebones.

What is a face but the thing that you see,
the symbol and fate of identity?

How would we recognize each from each:
a dog from a man — which face on a leash?

And when tears fall where no face is,
will the tears be mine or will they be his?

To select hot coal or gold no man is free,
each choice being determined by identity.

But exchange your face then what you choose
is gained, like love, by what you lose.

Now you twelve jurymen please retire,
put your right hands in ice and your left in fire.

A hole where the face was frightens us,
and a man who can choose is dangerous.

So what is your verdict going to be,
should he be hung from a gallows tree?

Oh some say high and some say low
to swing, swing, swing, when the free winds blow.

Verses at Night

Britain is to get a new air raid system . . . Priority will be to estimate which direction radioactive clouds will take. This will give farmers a chance to move livestock indoors and others to stock up food.

General Sir Sidney Kirkman,
Chief of Civil Defence
17th January 1956

Sleepless, by the windowpane I stare.
   Unseen aeroplanes disturb the air.
   The lazar moon glares down aghast.
     The seven branched tree is bare.

Could this be like Hiroshima's gruesome Past,
   each fly-skinned man to raw meat cursed,
   glow of the radioactive worm,
     this, our future of the Blast?

Unreal? East and West fat Neros yearn
   for other fiddled Romes to burn;
   and so dogma cancels dogma
     and heretics in their turn.

By my wife now, I lie quiet as a
   thought of how moon and stars might blur,
   and miles of smoke squirm overhead
     rising to Man's arbiter;

the grey skins shrivelling from the head,
   our two skulls in the double bed,
   leukaemia in the soul of all,
     flowing through the blood instead.

'No,' I cry as by her side I sprawl.
'No,' impotently, as I hear my small
dear daughter whimper in her cot
and across the darkness call.

Emperors of the Island

A political parable to be read aloud

There is the story of a deserted island
where five men walked down to the bay.

The story of this island is
that three men would two men slay.

Three men dug two graves in the sand,
three men stood on the sea wet rock,
three shadows moved away.

There is the story of a deserted island
where three men walked down to the bay.

The story of this island is
that two men would one man slay.

Two men dug one grave in the sand,
two men stood on the sea wet rock,
two shadows moved away.

There is the story of a deserted island
where two men walked down to the bay.

The story of this island is
that one man would one man slay.

One man dug one grave in the sand,
one man stood on the sea wet rock,
one shadow moved away.

There is the story of a deserted island
where four ghosts walked down to the bay.

The story of this island is
that four ghosts would one man slay.

Four ghosts dug one grave in the sand,
four ghosts stood on the sea wet rock;
five ghosts moved away.

Elegy for Dylan Thomas

All down the valleys they are talking,
    and in the community of the smoke-laden town.
Tomorrow, through bird trailed skies, across labouring waves,

wrong–again Emily will come to the dandelion yard
          and, with rum tourists, inspect his grave.

          Death was his voluntary marriage,
and his poor silence sold to that rich and famous bride.
          Beleaguered in that essential kiss he rode
the whiskey–meadows of her breath till, mortal, voiceless,
          he gave up his nailed ghost and he died.

          No more to celebrate
his disinherited innocence or your half–buried heart
          drunk as a butterfly, or sober as black.
Now, one second from earth, not even for the sake
          of love can his true energy come back.

          So cease your talking.
Too familiar you blaspheme his name and collected legends:
          some tears fall soundlessly and aren't the same
          as those that drop with obituary explosions.
          Suddenly, others who sing seem older and lame.

          But far from the blind country of prose,
wherever his burst voice goes about you or through you,
          look up in surprise, in a hurt public house
          or in a rain–blown street, and see how
          no fat ghost but a quotation cries.

          Stranger, he is laid to rest
not in the nightingale dark nor in the canary light.
          At the dear last, the yolk broke in his head,

blood of his soul's egg in a splash of bright
voices and now he is dead.

December, 1953

Enter The Movement

They said proudly, 'Our demon', pointing to
the Boat-house and the famous tenant who
sang in the night with half the lights put out.
Sometimes his song was true, no mere ranting shout.

Sensual intruders rejoiced and danced
to his gorgeous music and, if in time, it chanced
the ceiling sagged with sound and the walls cracked,
well, he sang the Welsh passion others lacked.

His powerful voice broke all the windows,
which transparencies must be paid in prose
not by wild fictions of a singing clown.
Some applauded when his roof fell down.

Then winter came when whistling beggars freeze.
He, to quench inner fires, drank catastrophes
while corybants, roaring, jigged with joy outside
till, delirious, that lyric singer died.

Now all cry, 'Regard that desperate ruin
of a life, example of Dionysian sin,'
and begin to rebuild, replace the roof,
finding one devil damnable enough.

The new choir that moves in is neat and sane
and dare not whistle in the dark again.
Proudly English, they sing with sharp, flat voices
but no-one dances, nobody rejoices.

The Moment

You raise your eyes from the level book
as if deeply listening. You are further than I call.
Like Eurydice you wear a hurt and absent look,
but I'm gentle for the silence into which you fall so sadly.
What are you thinking? Do you love me?
Suddenly you are not you at all but a ghost
dreaming of a castle to haunt or a heavy garden;
some place eerie, and far from me. But now a door
is banging outside, so you turn your head surprised.

You speak my name and someone else has died.

Anniversary

(At Primrose Hill, London)

The tree grows down from a bird.
The strong grass pulls up the earth
to a hill. Wade here, my dear,
through green shallows of daisies.
I hear the voice talking that is dead
behind the voice that is talking now.
The clocks of the smoky town
strike a quiet, grating sound.
Tomorrow will be the same.
Two sit on this hill and count
two moving from the two that stayed.

What happens to a flame blown out?
What perishes? Not this view,
nor my magnified hand in yours
whatever hurt and angers done.
I breathe in air the dead breathed out.
When first you inclined your face
to mine, my sweet ally came,
with your brown eyes purely wide.
My right hand on your left breast
I said, I have little to tell my dear.
For the pure bird, a pure cage.

Oh the silence that you lost
blind in the pandemonium
of the kiss and ruined was.
My dear, my dear, what perishes?
I hear this voice in a voice to come.

The Victim of Aulis

A multitude of masts in the harbour.
The sails limp in the air, becalmed.
The tired sea barely moving.
    The sea breathes quietly, Agamemnon.
        The wind is dead.
The sunlight leaping the waters,
the waters lapping at the boats.
Heat haze.
The King prowls the still deck
back and fore while the Captains quarrel.
We only throw dice and curse.
    The child! The child!
The whisper of the sea, the secret of the sea;
the sea is dreaming and a tall slave sings.
    What are we to do?
        They will think of a way.
            We have had nothing of education
                We must obey, being little men.
                The cause is just.
                    Leave it to the Captains.
                        What does Calchas say?
                            The child! The child!
And we thinking of our own daughters
with clumsy father-pride,
though those other virgins are faceless now
indistinct as the mingling of voices,
as the shuffle of the sea,
the little sound of the sea.
    It has been a long time.
        Leave it to the priests.
Conference at Aulis.

And he, the King, listening to the whisper of Calchas,
to the sea restless in its sleep while a tall slave sings –
sings of home and alien distances,
a slow voice, sad as a light,
as a flame burning in daytime.
Agamemnon is in religion.
It's that or nothing now.
The child! The child!
And she peering down through the fathomless minds
of the sea, at green shadows and dark dreams of fish –
for the deep thoughts of the sea are fish –
and she trailing her small hands in the waters
playing with coloured beads of spray.
Come with me.
Why father?
We sit on the stone quay with the sun and the seagulls.
We know nothing of rough mythologies, only facts.
We need the gods more than they need us.
And never again will some come home,
Artemis is offended, Calchas said,
staring at golden bangles spinning on the sea,
at arrows of poisoned sunlight pricking the flat sea;
the yellow masts vertical, pointing at the blue, indifferent sky,
the white sails lagging down, without life, without wind.
Calchas mumbles: Troy, Troy.
We only throw dice and curse the dawn we sailed away,
grumble and tell lewd tales of faithless women,
remembering Helen ravished in a foreign bed.
The child! The child!
And the King musing: what will her mother say?
The scandal and the sadness of it. And she who has no breasts

trailing her small hands in the waters, just a child,
still a child — that is a fearful thing.
    Come with me.
        Why father?
Murder at Aulis.
Oh the questions of the young-to-be-slain,
and the memory of black eyelashes pulled apart suddenly
revealing more white of the eye than a man bargained for.
The King is in religion
whose name is great among the Greeks —
the blood, ridiculously crimson in the groves of Artemis,
and the wind howling, why father? why father?
for many days and louder in the silence of the night,
and distressing him and possessing him in the mornings,
in the sea-spray climbing, and in the sea-howl,
as the fleet drags on aslant in the furious wind.
They thought of a way.
We are insignificant men
who follow and obey
as the cracked sails billow out half below the leaping sea,
as the tall slave sings why Father? why Father?

The Game

Follow the crowds to where the turnstiles click.
The terraces fill. *Hoompa*, blares the brassy band.
Saturday afternoon has come to Ninian Park

and, beyond the goal posts, in the Canton Stand
between black spaces, a hundred matches spark.

Waiting, we recall records, legendary scores:
Fred Keenor, Hardy, in a royal blue shirt.
The very names, sad as the old songs, open doors
before our time where someone else was hurt.
Now, like an injured beast, the great crowd roars.

The coin is spun. Here all is simplified,
and we are partisan who cheer the Good,
hiss at passing Evil. Was Lucifer offside?
A wing falls down when cherubs howl for blood.
Demons have agents: the Referee is bribed.

The white ball smacked the crossbar. Satan rose
higher than the others in the smoked brown gloom
to sink on grass in a ballet dancer's pose.
Again, it seems, we hear a familiar tune
not quite identifiable. A distant whistle blows.

Memory of faded games, the discarded years;
talk of Aston Villa, Orient, and the Swans.
Half-time, the band played the same military airs
as when the Bluebirds once were champions.
Round touchlines the same cripples in their chairs.

Mephistopheles had his joke. The honest team
dribbles ineffectively, no one can be blamed.
Infernal backs tackle, inside forwards scheme,

and if they foul us need we be ashamed?
Heads up! Oh for a Ted Drake, a Dixie Dean.

'Saved' or else, discontents, we are transferred
long decades back, like Faust must pay that fee.
The Night is early. Great phantoms in us stir
as coloured jerseys hover, move diagonally
on the damp turf, and our eidetic visions blur.

God sign our souls! Because the obscure staff
of Hell rule this world, jugular fans guessed
the result halfway through the second half,
and those who know the score just seem depressed.
Small boys swarm the field for an autograph.

Silent the stadium. The crowds have all filed out.
Only the pigeons beneath the roofs remain.
The clean programmes are trampled underfoot,
and natural the dark, appropriate the rain,
while, under lamp-posts, threatening newsboys shout.

The Abandoned

Du, Nachbar Gott . . .
　　　　R.M. Rilke

. . . thy absence doth excel
All distance known
　　　　George Herbert

I

God, when you came to our house
　　we let you in. Hunted,
　　　　we gave you succour,
　　　　　　bandaged your hands,
　　　　　　　　bathed your feet.

Wanting water we gave you wine.
Wanting bread we gave you meat.

Sometimes, God, you should recall
　　we are your hiding-place.
　　　　Take away these hands
　　　　　　and you would fall.

Outside, the afflicted pass.
　　We only have to call.
　　　　They would open you
　　　　　　with crutch and glass.

Who else then could we betray
　　if not you, the nearest?
　　　　God, how you watch us
　　　　　　and shrink away.

2

Never have we known you so transparent.
You stand against the curtain and wear
its exact design. And if a window opens
(like a sign) then is it you
or the colours which are blown apart?
As in a station, sitting in a carriage,
we wonder which of the waiting trains depart.

God, you can't help your presence
any more than the glassy air that lies
between tree and skies. No need to pass
through wave-lengths human ears can't sense.

We never hear the front door close when you are leaving.
Sometimes we question if you are there at all.
No need to be so self-effacing,
quiet as language of the roses
or moss upon a wall.

We have to hold our breath to hear you breathing.

3

Dear God in the end you had to go.
Dismissing you, your absence made us sane.
We keep the bread and wine for show.

The white horse galloped across the snow,
melted, leaving no hoofmarks in the rain.
Dear God, in the end, you had to go.

The winds of war and derelictions blow,
howling across the radioactive plain.
We keep the bread and wine for show.

Sometimes what we do not know we know –
in Armageddon town they write your name
dear God. In the end you had to go.

Yet boarding the last ship out we'd sorrow
that grape is but grape and grain is grain.
We keep the bread and wine for show.

Will world be leased to vulture and the crow?
Small lights upon the shore begin to wane.
Dear God in the end you had to go,
we keep the bread and wine for show.

4

They say, truant, you've vanished, address unknown,
that those who trusted you don't do so now
and, like the bereaved, feel empty and alone.

No wonder the plaudits for you grow fainter:
the George Herbert-like poems; the holy
plagiarism of each landscape painter.

And the congregations fewer for the sting of prayer,
all the fawning words, all the honeyless hum –
all for you, neighbour Gott. And you not there.

Still we call the Register. You're not excused.
Disease? Here sir. *Famine*? Present sir. *War*?
They say you fashioned us so who's accused?

5

Last night, awakened, did we hear you call?
Memory, father of tears, who was that knocking?
That incautious noise. Was there someone knocking?
Someone we once knew when we were small?

God, you have so many disguises. Once, we
from our dark bedroom cots, in mild fear,
could see how across the walls and ceiling
shadows of light would appear and flee.

This morning an omen downstairs on the floor,
a fallen picture frame. No homecoming,
no shadow of a shadow returning to stay,
no slow opening of a creaking door.

And our thoughts blank as an angel's mirror
since you, it seems, have travelled the other way
farther than all distance known, and further.

Public Library

Who, in the public library, one evening after rain,
amongst the polished tables and linoleum,
stands bored under blank light to glance at these pages?
Whose absent mood, like neon glowing in the night,
is conversant with wet pavements, nothing to do?

Neutral, the clock-watching girl stamps out the date,
a forced celebration, a posthumous birthday,
her head buttered by the drizzling library lamps;
yet the accident of words, too, can light the semi-dark
should the reader lead them home, generously journey,
later to return, perhaps leaving a bus ticket as a bookmark.

Who wrote in margins hieroglyphic notations,
that obscenity, deleted this imperfect line?
Read by whose hostile eyes, in what bed-sitting rooms,
in which rainy, dejected railway stations?

The Water Diviner

Late, I have come to a parched land
doubting my gift, if gift I have,
the inspiration of water
spilt, swallowed by the sand.

To hear once more water trickle,
to stand in a stretch of silence

the divining pen twisting in the hand:
sign of depths alluvial.

Water owns no permanent shape,
sags, is most itself in chaos;
now, under the shadow of the idol,
dry mouth and dry landscape.

No rain falls with a refreshing sound
to settle tubular in a well,
elliptical in a bowl. No grape
lusciously moulds it round.

Clouds have no constant resemblance
to anything, blown by a hot wind,
flying mirages; the blue background,
light constructions of chance.

To hold back chaos I transformed
amorphous mass: clay, fire, or cloud,
so that the agèd gods might dance
and golden structures form.

I should have built, plain brick on brick,
a water tower. The sun flies on
arid wastes, barren hells too warm
and me with a hazel stick!

Rivulets vanished in the dust
long ago, great compositions

vaporized, salt on the tongue so thick
that drinking still I thirst.

Repeated desert, recurring drought,
sometimes hearing water trickle,
sometimes not, I, by doubting first,
believe: believing, doubt.

Return to Cardiff

'Hometown'; well, most admit an affection for a city:
grey, tangled streets I cycled on to school, my first cigarette
in the back lane, and, fool, my first botched love affair.
First everything. Faded torments; self-indulgent pity.

The journey to Cardiff seemed less a return than a raid
on mislaid identities. Of course the whole locus smaller:
the mile-wide Taff now a stream, the castle not as in some black,
gothic dream, but a decent sprawl, a joker's toy façade.

Unfocused voices in the wind, associations, clues,
odds and ends, fringes caught, as when, after the doctor quit,
a door opened and I glimpsed the white, enormous face
of my grandfather, suddenly aghast with certain news.

Unable to define anything I can hardly speak,
and still I love the place for what I wanted it to be

as much as for what it unashamedly is
now for me, a city of strangers, alien and bleak.

Unable to communicate I'm easily betrayed,
uneasily diverted by mere sense reflections
like those anchored waterscapes that wander, alter, in the Taff,
hour by hour, as light slants down a different shade.

Illusory, too, that lost dark playground after rain,
the noise of trams, gunshots in what they once called Tiger Bay.
Only real this smell of ripe, damp earth when the sun comes out,
a mixture of pungencies, half exquisite and half plain.

No sooner than I'd arrived the other Cardiff had gone,
smoke in the memory, these but tinned resemblances,
where the boy I was not and the man I am not
met, hesitated, left double footsteps, then walked on.

Sunday Evening

Loved not for themselves those tenors who sing
arias from 'Aïda' on horned, tinny
gramophones – but because they take a man back
to a half forgotten thing.

We, transported by this evening loaded
with a song recorded by Caruso,

recall some other place, another time,
now charmingly outmoded.

What, for wrong motives, too often is approved
proves we once existed, becomes mere flattery
– then it's ourselves whom we are listening to,
and, by hearing, we are moved.

To know, haunted, this echo too will fade
with fresh alliteration of the leaves,
as more rain, indistinct, drags down the sky
like a sense of gloom mislaid.

Dear classic, melodic absences
how stringently debarred, kept out of mind,
till some genius on a gramophone
holes defences, breaks all fences.

What lives in a man and calls him back
and back through desolate Sunday evenings?
Indescribable, oh faint generic name:
sweet taste, bitter lack.

The French Master

Everyone in Class II at the Grammar School
had heard of Walter Bird, known as Wazo.

They said he'd behead each dullard and fool
or, instead, carve off a tail for the fun.

Wazo's cane buzzed like a bee in the air.
Quietly, quietly, in the desks of Form III
sneaky Wazo tweaked our ears and our hair.
Walter Wazo, public enemy No. 1.

Five feet tall, he married sweet Doreen Wall,
and combmarks furrowed his vaselined hair;
his hands still fluttered ridiculously small,
his eyes the colour of a poison bottle.

Who'd think he'd falter, poor love-sick Walter
as bored he read out *Lettres de mon Moulin*;
his mouth had begun to soften and alter,
and Class IV ribbed him as only boys can.

Perhaps through kissing his wife to a moan
had alone changed the shape of his lips,
till the habit of her mouth became his own:
no more Walter Wazo, enemy No. 1.

'Boy', he'd whine, 'yes, please decline the verb to have,'
in tones dulcet and mild as a girl.
'Sorry sir, can't sir, must go to the lav,'
whilst Wazo stared out of this world.

Till one day in May Wazo buzzed like a bee
and stung, twice, many a warm, inky hand;

he stormed through the form, a catastrophe,
returned to this world, No. 1.

Alas, alas, to the Vth Form's disgrace
nobody could quote Villon to that villain.
Again the nasty old mouth zipped on his face,
and not a weak-bladdered boy in the class.

Was Doreen being kissed by a Mr Anon?
Years later, I purred, 'Your dear wife, Mr Bird?'
Teeth bared, how he *glared* before stamping on;
and suddenly I felt sorry for the bastard.

After the Release of Ezra Pound

In Jerusalem I asked
the ancient Hebrew poets to forgive you,
and what would Walt Whitman have said
and Thomas Jefferson?   Paul Potts

In Soho's square mile of unoriginal sin
where the fraudulent neon lights haunt,
but cannot hide, the dinginess of vice,
the jeans and sweater boys spoke of Pound,
and you, Paul, repeated your question.

The chee-chee bums in Torino's laughed and
the virgins of St Martin's School of Art.

The corner spivs with their Maltese masks
loitered for the two o'clock result,
and those in the restaurants of Greek Street,
eating income tax, did not hear the laugh.

Gentle Gentile, you asked the question.
Free now (and we praise this) Pound could answer.
The strip lighting of Soho did not fuse,
no blood trickled from a certain book
down the immaculate shelves of Zwemmer's.
But the circumcised did not laugh.
The swart nudes in the backrooms put on clothes
and the doors of the French pub closed.

Pound did not hear the raw Jewish cry,
the populations committed to the dark
when he muttered through the microphones
of murderers. He, not I, must answer.

Because of the structures of a beautiful poet
you ask the man who is less than beautiful,
and wait in the public neurosis of Soho,
in the liberty of loneliness for an answer.

In the beer and espresso bars they talked
of Ezra Pound, excusing the silences of an old man,
saying there is so little time between
the parquet floors of an institution
and the boredom of the final box.

Why, Paul, if that ticking distance between
was merely a journey long enough
to walk the circumference of a Belsen,
Walt Whitman would have been eloquent,
and Thomas Jefferson would have cursed.

Spring, 1958

Red Balloon

It sailed across the startled town,
over chapels, over chimney-pots,
wind-blown above a block of flats
before it floated down.

Oddly, it landed where I stood,
and finding's keeping, as you know.
I breathed on it, I polished it,
till it shone like living blood.

It was my shame, it was my joy,
it brought me notoriety.
From all of Wales the rude boys came,
it ceased to be a toy.

I heard the girls of Cardiff sigh
when my balloon, my red balloon,

soared higher like a happiness
towards the dark blue sky.

Nine months since, have I boasted of
my unique, my only precious;
but to no one dare I show it now
however long they swear their love.

'It's a Jew's balloon,' my best friend cried,
'stained with our dear Lord's blood.'
'That I'm a Jew is true,' I said,
said I, 'that cannot be denied.'

'What relevance?' I asked, surprised,
'what's religion to do with this?'
'Your red balloon's a Jew's balloon,
let's get it circumcised.'

Then some boys laughed and some boys cursed,
some unsheathed their dirty knives;
some lunged, some clawed at my balloon,
but still it would not burst.

They bled my nose, they cut my eye,
half conscious in the street I heard,
'Give up, give up your red balloon.'
I don't know exactly why.

Father, bolt the door, turn the key,
lest those sad, brash boys return

to insult my faith and steal
my red balloon from me.

The Grand View

Mystics, in their far, erotic stance,
neglect our vulgar catastrophes.
I, with cadence, rhyme and assonance,
must pardon their oceanic trance,
their too saintlike immoralities.

For I, too, spellbound by the grand view,
flung through vistas from this windy hill,
am in pure love. I do not know who
it is that I love, but I would flow
into One invisible and still.

Though islanded and inspired by
the merely human, I sing back robes of air
to uncover my ego-plundered eye,
abandoning my apostasy,
no more to make a home out of despair.

Only Moses on the high mountain
at least knew what he was climbing for.
God-haunted, wonderstruck, half insane,

that condemned genius brought down again
ten social poems we call the law.

My littleness makes but a private sound,
the little lyric of a little man;
yet, like Moses, I walk on holy ground
since all earth is, and the world is round
I come back to where he began.

My forehead is open. The horns grow out
and exit. Infirm cynics knock inside,
and still ancestral voices shout
visions, visions! Should I turn about
if, by naming all, One is denied?

There are moments when a man must sing
of a lone Presence he cannot see.
To undulations of space I bring
all my love when love is happening;
green directions flying back to me.

There are moments when a man must praise
the astonishment of being alive,
when small mirrors of reality blaze
into miracles; and there's One always
who, by never departing, almost arrives.

Two Voices

A woman to a man

To own nothing, but to be —
like the vagrant wind that bears
faintest fragrance of the sea
or, in anger, lifts and tears
yet hoards no property;

I praise that state of mind:
wind, music, and you, are such.
All the visible you find
(the invisible you touch)
alter, and leave behind.

To pure being you devote
all your days. You are your eyes,
seemingly near but remote.
Gone, now, the sense of surprise,
like a dying musical note.

Like fragrance, you left no trace,
like anger, you came my way,
like music, you filled the space
(by going, the more you stay).
Departures were in your face.

2 *A wife to a husband*

Doth the music always flee?
Who kiss, that they may own,
sing happily, oh happily

44

of brick on brick till stone
keeps out both wind and sea.

So come back fast, come back slow,
I'll be distance and your home,
every symbol that I know,
church, tower, mosque, and dome,
then by staying, the more you'll go.

Let me breathe in music where
I am nothing but your life;
your designs, directions share,
to be no mistress but a wife,
pluck your meanings from the air.

I'll be all things you would be,
the four winds and the seven seas,
you'll play with such a gaiety
devastating melodies
till music be my body.

From a Suburban Window

Such afternoon glooms, such clouds chimney low —
London, the clouds want to move but can not,
London, the clouds want to rain but can not —
such negatives of a featureless day;

the street empty but for a van passing,
an afternoon smudged by old afternoons.
Soon, despite railings, evening will come
from a great distance trailing evenings.
Meantime, unemployed sadness loiters here.

Quite suddenly, six mourners appear:
a couple together, then three stout men,
then one more, lagging behind, bare-headed.
Not one of the six looks up at the sky,
and not one of them touches the railings.
They walk on and on remembering days,
yet seem content. They employ the décor.
They use this grey inch of eternity,
and the afternoon, so praised, grows distinct.

Close Up

Often you seem to be listening to a music
that others cannot hear. Rilke would have loved you:
you never intrude, you never ask questions
of those, crying in the dark, who are most near.

You always keep something of yourself to yourself
in the electric bars, even in bedrooms.
Rilke would have praised you: your nearness is far,
and, therefore, your distance like the very stars.

Yet some things you miss and some things you lose
by keeping your arm outstretched; and some things
you'll never know unless one, at least, knows you
like a close-up, in detail – blow by human blow.

As I Was Saying

Yes, madam, as a poet I *do* take myself seriously,
and, since I have a young, questioning family, I suppose
I should know something about English wild flowers:
the shape of their leaves, when this and that one grows,
how old mythologies attribute strange powers
to this or that one. Urban, I should mug up anew
the pleasant names: Butterbur, Ling, and Lady's Smock,
Jack-by-the Hedge, Cuckoo-Pint, and Feverfew,
even the Stinking Hellebore – all in that W. H. Smith book
I could bring home for myself (inscribed to my daughter)
to swot, to know which is this and which that one,
what honours the high cornfield, what the low water,
under the slow-pacing clouds and occasional sun of England.

   But no! Done for in the ignorant suburb,
I'll drink Scotch, neurotically stare through glass
at the rainy lawn, at green stuff, nameless birds,
and let my daughter, madam, go to nature class.
I'll not compete with those nature poets you advance,

some in country dialect, and some in dialogue
with the country – few as calm as their words:
Wordsworth, Barnes, sad John Clare who ate grass.

Olfactory Pursuits

Often, unobserved, I smell my own hand.
I am searching for something forgotten.
I bang the door behind me, breathing in.

I think that a bitter or candied scent
is like a signpost pointing backwards
on which is writ no place and no distance.

So I walk towards a Verulamium,
your ruins or my ruins. The sun's ambushed:
fleeing on the ground the same, large shadow.

Look up. There's no smell to the colour blue.
The wind blew it right through the spaces
between clouds. Christ, what is it I'm after?

I dream, without sleeping, of things obscure,
of houses and streets and temples deserted
which, if once visited, I don't recall.

Here are a few stones instead of a wall,
and here broken stones instead of a house.
Hopelessly, with odours I conjoin.

My footfall echoes down old foundations,
buried mosaics, tomb tablets crumbled,
flints in the grass, your ruins or my ruins.

A man sniffs the back of his own hand,
moistens it with his mouth, to sniff again,
to think a blank; writes, 'The odour of stones.'

Pathology of Colours

I know the colour rose, and it is lovely,
but not when it ripens in a tumour;
and healing greens, leaves and grass, so springlike,
in limbs that fester are not springlike.

I have seen red-blue tinged with hirsute mauve
in the plum-skin face of a suicide.
I have seen white, china white almost, stare
from behind the smashed windscreen of a car.

And the criminal, multi-coloured flash
of an H-bomb is no more beautiful

than an autopsy when the belly's opened –
to show cathedral windows never opened.

So in the simple blessing of a rainbow,
in the bevelled edge of a sunlit mirror,
I have seen, visible, Death's artefact
like a soldier's ribbon on a tunic tacked.

Hunt the Thimble

Hush now. You cannot describe it.

Is it like heavy rain falling,
and lights going on, across the fields,
in the new housing estate?

Cold, cold. Too domestic, too
temperate, too devoid of history.

Is it like a dark windowed street at night,
the houses uncurtained, the street deserted?

Colder. You are getting colder,
and too romantic, too dream-like.
You cannot describe it.

The brooding darkness then
that breeds inside a cathedral
of a provincial town in Spain.

In Spain, also, but not Spanish.
In England, if you like, but not English.
It remains, even when obscure, perpetually.
Aged, but ageless, you cannot describe it.
No, you are cold, altogether too cold.

Aha – the blue sky over Ampourias,
the blue sky over Lancashire for that matter . . .

You cannot describe it.

. . . obscured by clouds?
I must know what you mean.

Hush, hush.

Like those old men in hospital dying,
who, unaware strangers stand around their bed,
stare obscurely, for a long moment,
at one of their own hands raised –
which perhaps is bigger than the moon again –
and then, drowsy, wandering, shout out, 'Mama'.

Is it like that? Or hours after that even:
the darkness inside a dead man's mouth?

No, no, I have told you:
you are cold, and you cannot describe it.

A Night Out

Friends recommended the new Polish film
at the Academy in Oxford Street.
So we joined the ever melancholy queue
of cinemas. A wind blew faint suggestions
of rain towards us, and an accordion.
Later, uneasy, in the velvet dark
we peered through the cut-out oblong window
at the spotlit drama of our nightmares:
images of Auschwitz almost authentic,
the human obscenity in close-up.
Certainly we could imagine the stench.

Resenting it, we forgot the barbed wire
was but a prop and could not scratch an eye;
those striped victims merely actors like us.
We saw the Camp orchestra assembled,
we heard the solemn gaiety of Bach,
scored by the loud arrival of an engine,
its impotent cry and its guttural trucks.
We watched, as we munched milk chocolate,
trustful children, no older than our own,

strolling into the chambers without fuss,
while smoke, black and curly, oozed from chimneys.

Afterwards, at a loss, we sipped coffee
in a bored espresso bar nearby
saying very little. You took off one glove.
Then to the comfortable suburb swiftly
where, arriving home, we garaged the car.
We asked the au pair girl from Germany
if anyone had phoned at all, or called,
and, of course, if the children had woken.
Reassured, together we climbed the stairs,
undressed together, and naked together,
in the dark, in the marital bed, made love.

Fah

Not to irritate him did you sit,
frequenting one note, at the piano stool,
over and over; resting your finger
on that one sound till that sound vanished.
Yes, you played it again after it faded,
then felt it again and played it again
as he became anxious, a tightening nerve.

For that one sound, at first amiable,
soon touched down on the whole feminine,

far world of hermetic lamentations.
You sat there, it seemed, absent, unaware,
like a child (certainly without menace)
and fathomed it again and played it again,
a small desperation this side of death.

Not to confront him with choices
did you play: he did not quit the room quietly;
he did not shout out abruptly, 'Stop it';
he would not say with compassion, 'My dear . . .';
but only coughed behind his hand politely.
Odd, then, that he coughed again and again,
and could not stop although the tears came.

Even

Coffee-time morning, down the gradient,
like a shop window for Jehovah,
they pass my gate to the synagogue
as Saturday skies vault over.

Dressed like that they lose their charm
who carry prayer books, wear a hat.
I don't like them, I don't like them,
and guilty fret – just thinking that.

I don't like them, I don't like them –
again the dodgy thought comes through:
could it be I am another
tormented, anti-semite Jew?

No. Next morning on the Sunday,
processions uphill, piebald, lurch,
in the opposite direction,
towards the ivy-covered church.

Look, dressed for Christ and hygiene,
they glare back like Swiss-Germans
spruced and starched in piety,
and fag on slow as sermons.

All God's robots lose their charm
who carry prayer books, wear a hat.
I don't like them, I don't like them,
and feel less guilty thinking that.

So let both ministers propound
the pathology of religions,
and pass my gate you zealots of
scrubbed, schizophrenic visions.

The Ballad of Oedipus Sex

I pull the knife out of my chest,
    the light begins to fail.
  Don't read the Sunday papers:
    myself will tell the tale.
Forget the printed photograph
    that makes me look a freak.
  Oedipus wrote the headlines
    for longer than a week,

    singing hey diddle diddlio,
      hey diddle diddle dee.

It was midnight on the river,
    the sky a domino.
  I pushed my gloomy father
    into gloomy coils below.
Such a silence on the river,
    you could hear the oars creak.
  Oedipus wrote the headlines
    for longer than a week,

    singing hey diddle diddlio,
      hey diddle diddle dee.

I rowed straight home to stepmother
    and seized her in my bed.
  A moth was in the lampshade,
    the light was in my head:
some like girls contemporary
    but I like them antique.

Oedipus wrote the headlines
    for longer than a week,

        singing hey diddle diddlio,
            hey diddle diddle dee.

When, dripping, the ghost of father,
    a hatchet in his hand,
appeared on the threshold
    I found I couldn't stand;
though true love may last forever
    for me it turned out bleak.
Oedipus wrote the headlines
    for longer than a week,

        singing hey diddle diddlio,
            hey diddle diddle dee.

I telephoned the analyst
    and conned him for a date.
He listened to my dreaming,
    a father surrogate.
I arose and cut his throat then
    from bloody cheek to cheek.
Oedipus wrote the headlines
    for longer than a week,

        singing hey diddle diddlio,
            hey diddle diddle dee.

The analyst had a lady,
    she never said a word;
  for when I gazed into her eyes
    a transference occurred.
So I took her to the river
    and now she's up the creek.
  Oedipus wrote the headlines
    for longer than a week,

    singing hey diddle diddlio,
      hey diddle diddle dee.

Six policemen came a-knocking,
    the door they tried to force.
  I'd have horsewhipped the lot if
    I'd only had a horse.
Six bullets through the keyhole,
    six policemen sprung a leak.
  Oedipus wrote the headlines
    for longer than a week,

    singing hey diddle diddlio,
      hey diddle diddle dee.

I was sheltered by Jocasta,
    a widow with catarrh.
  'Your sins be white as snow,' she thrilled,
    'Long as you love your ma.
Forget my past, my pet, my poodle,
    and let me be your peke.'

Oedipus wrote the headlines
　　for longer than a week,

　　singing hey diddle diddlio,
　　　hey diddle diddle dee.

So of Jocasta now I sing
　　like any swooning bard:
the very wrinkles of her face,
　　her arteries so hard.
Mock if you must! You don't know her!
　　Or her veteran's technique.
Oedipus wrote the headlines
　　for longer than a week,

　　singing hey diddle diddlio,
　　　hey diddle diddle dee.

A son we had and loved him,
　　I loved him more than best;
but on his thirteenth birthday
　　he knifed me in the chest.
At the Golden Cock in Fleet Street
　　they tell how Greek met Greek.
Oedipus wrote the headlines
　　for longer than a week,

　　singing hey diddle diddlio,
　　　hey diddle diddle dee.

Since Sophocles and Shakespeare
        divined our human laws,
    I've gone bleeding down the aisles
        to inTERminable applause.
Now I'm dying, Jocasta, dying,
        my plot was not unique:
    Oedipus wrote the headlines
        for longer than a week,

        singing hey diddle diddlio,
            hey diddle diddle . . . Dada?

Not Adlestrop

Not Adlestrop, no – besides, the name
hardly matters. Nor did I languish in June heat.
Simply, I stood, too early, on the empty platform,
and the wrong train came in slowly, surprised, stopped.
Directly facing me, from a window,
a very, *very* pretty girl leaned out.

        When I, all instinct,
stared at her, she, all instinct, inclined her head away
as if she'd divined the much married life in me,
or as if she might spot, up platform,
some unlikely familiar.

For my part, under the clock, I continued
my scrutiny with unmitigated pleasure.
And she knew it, she certainly knew it, and would not
glance at me in the silence of not Adlestrop.

Only when the train heaved noisily, only
when it jolted, when it slid away, only *then*,
daring and secure, she smiled back at my smile,
and I, daring and secure, waved back at her waving.
And so it was, all the way down the hurrying platform
as the train gathered atrocious speed
towards Oxfordshire or Gloucestershire.

In Llandough Hospital

'To hasten night would be humane,'
I, a doctor, beg a doctor,
for still the darkness will not come –
his sunset slow, his first star pain.

I plead: 'We know another law.
For one maimed bird we'd do as much,
and if a creature need not suffer
must he, for etiquette, endure?'

Earlier, 'Go now, son,' my father said,
for my sake commanding me.

Now, since death makes victims of us all,
he's thin as Auschwitz in that bed.

Still his courage startles me. The fears
I'd have, he has none. Who'd save
Socrates from the hemlock,
or Winkelried from the spears?

We quote or misquote in defeat,
in life, and at the camps of death.
Here comes the night with all its stars,
bright butchers' hooks for man and meat.

I grasp his hand so fine, so mild,
which still is warm surprisingly,
not a handshake either, father,
but as I used to when a child.

And as a child can't comprehend
what germinates philosophy,
so like a child I question why
night with stars, then night without end.

The Motto

Who heard the no thing to write nothing down?
Who switched the record player on instead?

Whose slate-blue smoke idled to the lampshade?
Who killed his cigarette and went to bed?

Who, half the night, could not sleep for Mozart
And thought to hell with all those classic gems?

Who said without such music in the head
A man's more fit for stratagems?

He bungled though – when music sought him out.
He whistled still, but did not know what for.

His stick in winter doodled in the snow;
Be visited, expect nothing, and endure.

The Smile Was

I

one thing I waited for always
after the shouting
after the palaver
the perineum stretched to pain
the parched voice of the midwife
        Push! Push!
and I can't and the rank
sweet smell of the gas

and
         I can't
as she whiffed cotton wool
inside her head
as the hollow stones of gas
dragged
      her
         down
from the lights above
to the river-bed, to the real stones.
              Push! Push!
as she floated up again
muscles tensed, to the electric
till the little head was crowned;
and I shall wait again
for the affirmation.

For it is such:
that effulgent, tender, satisfied
smile of a woman
who, for the first time,
hears the child crying the world
for the very first time.

That agreeable, radiant smile —
no man can smile it
no man can paint it
as it develops without fail,
after the gross, physical, knotted,
granular, bloody endeavour.
    Such a pure spirituality, from all that!

It occupies the face
and commands it.
          Out of relief
you say, reasonably thinking of the reasonable,
swinging lightness of any reprieve,
the joy of it, almost helium in the head.

          So wouldn't you?
And truly there's always the torture of the unknown.
There's always the dream of pregnant women,
blood of the monster in the blood of the child;
and we all know of generations lost
like words faded on a stone,
of minds blank or wild with genetic mud.
          And couldn't you
smile like that?
Not like that, no, never,
not with such indefinable
dulcitude as that.
And so she smiles
with eyes as brown as a dog's
or eyes blue-mad as a doll's
it makes no odds
whore, beauty, or bitch,
it makes no odds
illimitable chaste happiness
in that smile
as new life-in-the-world
for the first time cries the world.
No man can smile like that.

2

No man can paint it.
Da Vinci sought it out
yet was far, far, hopelessly.
Leonardo, you only made
Mona Lisa look six months gone!
I remember the smile of the Indian.
I told him
          Fine, finished,
you are cured
and he sat there smiling sadly.
Any painter could paint it
the smile of a man resigned
saying
          Thank you, doctor,
you have been kind
and then, as in melodrama,
          How long
have I to live?
The Indian smiling, resigned,
all the fatalism of the East.

So one starts again, also smiling,
          All is well
you are well, you are cured.
And the Indian still smiling
his assignations with death
still shaking his head, resigned.
          Thank you
for telling me the truth, doctor.

Two months? Three months?
And beginning again
    and again
whatever I said, thumping the table,
however much I reassured him
the more he smiled the conspiratorial
smile of a damned, doomed man.

Now a woman, a lady, a whore,
a bitch, a beauty, whatever,
    the child's face crumpled
as she becomes the mother,
she smiles differently, ineffably.

3

As different as
the smile of my colleague,
his eyes reveal it,
his ambiguous assignations,
good man, good surgeon,
whose smile arrives of its own accord
    from nowhere
like flies to a dead thing
when he makes the first incision.
Who draws a line of blood
across the soft, white flesh
as if something beneath,
desiring violence, had beckoned him;
who draws a ritual wound,
a calculated wound

to heal – to heal,
but still a wound –
good man, good surgeon,
his smile as luxuriant
as the smile of Peter Lorre.

So is the smile of my colleague,
the smile of a man
secretive behind the mask.

The smile of war.

But the smile, the smile
of the new mother,
what
   an extraordinary
      open thing
         it is.

4

Walking home tonight I saw
an ordinary occurrence
hardly worth remarking on:
an unhinged star, a streaking gas,
and I thought how lovely
destruction is when it is far.
Ruined it slid
on the dead dark towards fiction:
its lit world disappeared

phut, through one punched hole or another,
slipped unseen down the back of the sky
into another time.

Never,
not for one single death
can I forget we die with the dead,
and the world dies with us;
yet
in one, lonely,
small child's birth
all the tall dead rise
to break the crust of the imperative earth.

No wonder the mother smiles
a wonder like that,
a lady, a whore, a bitch, a beauty.
Eve smiled like that
when she heard Seth cry out Abel's dark,
earth dark, the first dark
eeling on the deep sea-bed,
struggling on the real stones.
Hecuba, Cleopatra, Lucretia Borgia,
Annette Vallon smiled like that.

They all, still, smile like that,
when the child first whimpers like a seagull
the ancient smile reasserts itself
instinct with a return
so outrageous and so shameless;
the smile the smile

always the same
      an uncaging
           a freedom.

Mysteries

At night, I do not know who I am
when I dream, when I am sleeping.

Awakened, I hold my breath and listen:
a thumbnail scratches the other side of the wall.

At midday, I enter a sunlit room
to observe the lamplight on for no reason.

I should know by now that few octaves can be heard,
that a vision dies from being too long stared at;

that the whole of recorded history even
is but a little gossip in a great silence;

that a magnesium flash cannot illumine,
for one single moment, the invisible.

I do not complain. I start with the visible
and am startled by the visible.

Forgotten

That old country I once said I'd visit
when older. Can no one tell me its name?
Odd to have forgotten what it is called.
I would recognize the name if I heard it.
So many times I have searched the atlas
with a prowling convex lens – to no avail.

I know the geography of the great world
has changed; the war, the peace, the deletions
of places – red pieces gone forever,
and names of countries altered forever:
Gold Coast Ghana, Persia become Iran,
Siam Thailand, and Hell now Vietnam.

People deleted. Must I sleep again to reach it,
to find the back door opening to a field,
a barking of dogs, and a path that leads back?
One night in pain, the dead middle of night,
will I awake again, know who I am,
the man from somewhere else, and the place's name?

An Old Commitment

Long ago my kinsmen slain in battle,
swart flies on all their pale masks feeding.

I had a cause then. Surely I had a cause?
I was for them and they were for me.

Now, when I recall why, what, who,
I think the thought that is as blank as stone.

Travelling this evening, I focus on the back
of brightness, on that red spot wavering.

Behind it, what have I forgotten? It goes
where the red spot goes, rising, descending.

I only describe a sunset, a car travelling
on a swerving mountain road, that's all.

Arriving too late, I approach the unlit dark.
Those who loiter outside exits and entrances

so sadly, so patiently, even they have departed.
And I am no ghost and this place is in ruins.

'Black,' I call softly to one dead but beloved,
'black, black,' wanting the night to reply . . .
                                    . . . 'Black.'

Demo against the Vietnam War, 1968

Praise just one thing in London, he challenged,
as if everybody, everything, owned a minus,
was damnable, and the Inner Circle led to hell;
and I thought, allowed one slot only,
what, in October, would I choose?

Not the blurred grasslands of a royal, moody park
where great classy trees lurk in mist;
not the secretive Thames either, silvering
its slow knots through the East End –
sooty scenes, good for Antonioni panning soft
atmospheric shots, emblems of isolation,
prologue to the elegiac Square, the house where,
suddenly, lemon oblongs spring to windows.

Nor would I choose the stylized catalogue
of torment in the National Gallery.
Better that tatty group under Nelson's column,
their home-made banners held aloft,
their small cries of 'Peace, Peace,' impotent;
also the moment with the tannoy turned off,
the thudding wings of pigeons audible,
the shredding fountains, once again, audible.

So praise to the end of the march,
their songs, their jargon, outside the Embassy.
Yes, this I'd choose: their ardour, their naïveté,
violence of commitment, cruelty of devotion,
'We shall not be moved, We shall overcome' –
despite sullen police concealed in vans

waiting for arclights to fail, for furtive darkness,
and camera-teams, dismantled, all breezing home.

Peachstone

I do not visit his grave. He is not there.
Out of hearing, out of reach. I miss him here,
seeing hair grease at the back of a chair
near a firegrate where his spit sizzled,
or noting, in the cut-glass bowl, a peach.

For that night his wife brought him a peach,
his favourite fruit, while the sick light glowed,
and his slack, dry mouth sucked, sucked, sucked,
with dying eyes closed – perhaps for her sake –
till bright as blood the peachstone showed.

Three Street Musicians

Three street musicians in mourning overcoats
worn too long, shake money boxes this morning,
then, afterwards, play their suicide notes.

The violinist in chic, black spectacles, blind,
the stout tenor with a fake Napoleon stance,
and the loony flautist following behind,

they try to importune us, the busy living,
who hear melodic snatches of music hall
above unceasing waterfalls of traffic.

Yet if anything can summon back the dead
it is the old-time sound, old obstinate tunes,
such as they achingly render and suspend:

'The Minstrel Boy', 'Roses of Picardy'.
No wonder cemeteries are full of silences
and stones keep down the dead that they defend.

Stones too light! Airs irresistible!
Even a dog listens, one paw raised, while the stout,
loud man amazes with nostalgic notes – though half boozed

and half clapped out. And, as breadcrumbs thrown
on the ground charm sparrows down from nowhere,
now, suddenly, there are too many ghosts about.

Portrait of the Artist as a Middle-Aged Man

(3.30 a.m., January 1st)

Pure Xmas card below – street under snow,
under lamplight. My children curl asleep,
my wife also moans from depths too deep
with all her shutters closed and half her life.
And I? I, sober now, come down the stairs
to eat an apple, to taste the snow in it,
to switch the light on at the maudlin time.

Habitual living room, where the apple-flesh
turns brown after the bite, oh half my life
has gone to pot. And, now, too tired for sleep,
I count up the Xmas cards childishly,
assessing, *Jesus*, how many friends I've got!

A New Diary

This clerk-work, this first January chore
of who's in, who's out. A list to think about
when absences seem to shout, Scandal! Outrage!
So turning to the blank, prefatory page
I transfer most of the names and phone tags
from last year's diary. True, Meadway, Speedwell,
Mountview, are computer-changed into numbers,
and already their pretty names begin to fade

like Morwenna, Julie, Don't-Forget-Me-Kate,
grassy summer girls I once swore love to.
These, whispering others and time will date.

Cancelled, too, a couple someone else betrayed,
one man dying, another mind in rags.
And remembering them my clerk-work flags,
bitterly flags, for all lose, no-one wins,
those in, those out, *this* at the heart of things?
So I stop, ask: whom should I commemorate,
and who, perhaps, is crossing out my name now
from some future diary? Oh my God,
Morwenna, Julie, don't forget me, Kate.

The Death of Aunt Alice

Aunt Alice's funeral was orderly,
each mourner correct, dressed in decent black,
not one balding relative berserk with an axe.
Poor Alice, where's your opera-ending?
For alive you relished high catastrophe,
your bible Page One of a newspaper.

You talked of typhoid when we sat to eat;
Fords on the M4, mangled, upside down,
just when we were going for a spin;
and, at London airport, as you waved us off,

how you fatigued us with 'metal fatigue',
vague shapes of Boeings bubbling under seas.

Such disguises and such transformations!
Even trees were but factories for coffins,
rose bushes decoys to rip boys' eyes with thorns.
Sparrows became vampires, spiders had designs,
and your friends also grew SPECTACULAR,
none to bore you by dying naturally.

A. had both kidneys removed in error
at Guy's. 'And such a clever surgeon too.'
B., one night, fell screaming down a liftshaft.
'Poor fellow, he never had a head for heights.'
C., so witty, so feminine, 'Pity
she ended up in a concrete mixer.'

But now, never again, Alice, will you utter
gory admonitions as some do oaths.
Disasters that lit your eyes will no more
unless, trembling up there, pale saints listen
to details of their bloody martyrdoms,
all their tall stories, your eternity.

Car Journeys

1   *Down the M4*

Me! dutiful son going back to South Wales, this time afraid
to hear my mother's news. Too often, now, her friends are
    disrobed,
and my aunts and uncles, too, go into the hole, one by one.
The beautiful face of my mother is in its ninth decade.

Each visit she tells me the monotonous story of clocks.
'Oh dear,' I say, or 'how funny,' till I feel my hair turning grey
for I've heard that perishable one two hundred times before –
like the rugby 'amateurs' with golden sovereigns in their socks.

Then the Tawe ran fluent and trout-coloured over stones stonier,
more genuine; then Annabella, my mother's mother, spoke Welsh
with such an accent the village said, 'Tell the truth, fach,
you're no Jewess. *They're* from the Bible. *You're* from Patagonia!'

I'm driving down the M4 again under bridges that leap
over me then shrink in my side mirror. Ystalyfera is farther
than smoke and God further than all distance known. I whistle
no hymn but an old Yiddish tune my mother knows.
It won't keep.

2   *Driving home*

Opposing carbeams wash my face.
Such flickerings hypnotize. To keep awake
I listen to the BBC through cracklings
of static, fade-outs under bridges,
to a cool expert who, in lower case,

computes and graphs 'the ecological
disasters that confront the human race.'

Almost immediately (ironically?),
I see blue flashing lights ahead and brake
before a car accordioned, floodlit, men heaving
at a stretcher, an ambulance oddly angled, tame, in wait.
Afterwards, silent, I drive home cautiously
where, late, the eyes of my youngest child
flicker dreamily, and are full of television.

'He's waited up,' his mother says, 'to say goodnight.'
My son smiles briefly. Such emotion! I surprise
myself and him when I hug him tight.

A Note Left on the Mantelpiece

(For his wife)

Attracted by their winning names I chose
Little Yid and *Welsh Bard*; years later backed
the swanky jockeys, and still thought I lacked
inspiration, the uncommon touch, not
mere expertise. Each way, I paid in prose.

Always the colours and stadiums beckoned
till, on the nose, at Goodwood, the high gods
jinxed the favourite despite the odds.

Addict that I was, live fool and dead cert.
His velvet nostrils lagged a useless second.

A poet should have studied style not form
(sweet, I regret the scarcity of roses)
but by Moses and by the nine Muses
I'll no more. Each cruising nag is a beast
so other shirts can keep the centaur warm.

Adieu, you fading furlongs of boozing,
hoarse voices at Brighton, white rails, green course.
Conclusion? Why, not only the damned horse
but whom it's running against matters.
By the way, apologies for losing.

A Faithful Wife

*(A letter written by an Egyptian lady during the reign of
Amenhotep III, about 1385 BCE)*

To my husband, my lord,
whose caravans lodge in Canaan,
whose sperm has not stiffened,
for three long months, my bed-linen,
say:
at the feet of my husband,
as before the king, the sun-god,
seven times and seven times

I fall.
For I am an obedient
of my husband, my lord.

When I keep my head still
moving my two eyes this way
it is dark;
when I keep my head still
moving my two eyes that way
it is dark;
but when I gaze in front,
towards my lord, it is dazzle,
it is the spirit on the wall
flat as a sunbeam:
it is the time of the short shadows.

Further: all seems tasteless
like the white of an egg
since my lord departed.
Thus ask my falcon, my husband,
to send for his servant, as promised,
to journey on the stony heat
across the camel-coloured desert
even to the shrewd wells.
For I have placed the yoke
of my husband, my lord,
upon my neck and I bear it.

In the whirling dust-storm,
a brick may move

from beneath its companions.
When the night grows with jackals
a dog may move
from his sick master.
But send for me and I shall not move
from beneath the shadow
of my husband, my lord,
as that shadow will not move
from his two feet.

Yet my lord sends no report,
neither good nor evil.
Has he gone to the land of Hatti,
or to the region of the bedouins?
Does he take care of his chariot?
When the first three stars appear
does he sleep each evening
with a piece of wool upon him?
Or has the foe raided his caravans,
the night guards drunk, my lord inert?
Very anxious is thy servant.

Oh may this tablet find him safe
in Joppa, in the meadows
blossoming in their season:
else let the dust follow his chariot
like smoke, and let the god, Amon, keep
all those tracks that zag between
the rising and the setting sun
free from ambuscade,

free for my lord whose speeches are
gathered together on my tongue,
and remain upon my lips.

The Bereaved

1

Once his voice had been so thrilling,
the twelve women all agreed. Off and on TV
he was charming, he was charismatic,
yet without side. He was their pin-up.

But now his incomprehensible language
when he spoke (which was rare);
the way he would stare into chasms of space
as if Eurydice were there; or would suddenly

howl out an emptiness – that was too much
(a man should not dream of maggots too long)
that was ridiculous, even frightening, they said,
the twelve women, reasonably moving towards him.

2

Twelve women pulling him,
twelve women screaming,
kicking, scratching, pulling at him,

until on the ground, at last,
he was being smothered,
bitten by women's teeth,
his eyes pushed in by women's thumbs.

Afterwards, the cyanosed figure
on the ground, what was left of him,
striped with blood, did not move,
and the women stood back silent,
most of them already smoking
and the others lighting up.

In the Theatre

(A true incident)

Only a local anaesthetic was given because of the blood pressure problem. The patient, thus, was fully awake throughout the operation. But in those days – in 1938, in Cardiff, when I was Lambert Rogers' dresser – they could not locate a brain tumour with precision. Too much normal brain tissue was destroyed as the surgeon crudely searched for it, before he felt the resistance of it . . . all somewhat hit and miss. One operation I shall never forget . . .

Dr Wilfred Abse

Sister saying – 'Soon you'll be back in the ward,'
sister thinking – 'Only two more on the list,'

the patient saying – 'Thank you, I feel fine';
small voices, small lies, nothing untoward,
though, soon, he would blink again and again
because of the fingers of Lambert Rogers,
rash as a blind man's, inside his soft brain.

If items of horror can make a man laugh
then laugh at this: one hour later, the growth
still undiscovered, ticking its own wild time;
more brain mashed because of the probe's braille path;
Lambert Rogers desperate, fingering still;
his dresser thinking, 'Christ! Two more on the list,
a cisternal puncture and a neural cyst.'

Then, suddenly, the cracked record in the brain,
a ventriloquist voice that cried, 'You sod,
leave my soul alone, leave my soul alone,' –
the patient's dummy lips moving to that refrain,
the patient's eyes too wide. And, shocked,
Lambert Rogers drawing out the probe
with nurses, students, sister, petrified.

'Leave my soul alone, leave my soul alone,'
that voice so arctic and that cry so odd
had nowhere else to go – till the antique
gramophone wound down and the words began
to blur and slow, '. . . leave . . . my . . . soul . . . alone . . .'
to cease at last when something other died.
And silence matched the silence under snow.

Funland

1   *The superintendent*

With considerable poise
the superintendent
has been sitting for hours now
at the polished table.
Outside the tall window
all manner of items
have been thundering down
boom boom stagily
the junk of heaven.

A harp with the nerves missing
the somewhat rusty
sheet iron wings of an angel
a small bent tubular hoop
still flickering flickering
like fluorescent lighting
when first switched on
that old tin lizzie banger
Elijah's burnt-out chariot
various other religious hardware
and to cap it all
you may not believe this
a red Edwardian pillar box.

My atheist uncle has been standing
in the corner wrathfully.
Fat Blondie in her pink
transparent nightdress
has been kneeling

on the brown linoleum.
And for some queer reason
our American guest yells
from time to time Mari-*an*
if they give you chewing gum
. . . . CHEW.

Meanwhile the superintendent
a cautious man usually
inclined for instance
to smile in millimetres
has begun to take a great risk.

Calm as usual
masterful as usual
he is drawing the plans of the void
working out its classical proportions.

2   *Anybody here seen any Thracians?*

The tall handsome man
whom the superintendent
has nicknamed Pythagoras
asked fat Blondie
as she reclined strategically
under the cherry blossom
to join his Society.

The day after that
despite initial fleerings
my uncle also agreed.

The day following another hundred.
Two more weeks everyone
had signed on the dotted line.

There are very few rules.
Members promise to abstain
from swallowing beans. They promise
not to pick up what has fallen
never to stir a fire with an iron
never to eat the heart of animals
never to walk on motorways
never to look in a mirror
that hangs beside a light.
All of us are happy with the rules.

But Pythagoras is not happy.
He wanted to found
a Society not a Religion
and a Society he says
washing his hands with moonlight
in a silver bowl
has to be exclusive.
Therefore someone must be banned.
Who? Who? Tell us Pythagoras.
The Thracians yes the Thracians.

But there are no Thracians among us.
We look left and right wondering
who of us could be a secret Thracian
wondering
who of us would say

with the voice of insurrection
I love you
not in a bullet proof room
and not with his eyes closed.

Pythagoras also maintains
that Thracians have blue hair and red eyes.
Now all day we loiter near the gates
hoping to encounter someone of this description
so that what is now a Religion
can triumphantly become a Society.

3   *The summer conference*

On grassy lawns
modern black-garbed priests
and scientists in long white coats
confer and dally.
Soon the superintendent will begin
his arcane disquisition
on the new bizarre secret weapon.
(Psst – the earwigs of RAF Odiham)
Meanwhile I – surprise surprise –
observe something rather remarkable
over there.

Nobody else sees it (near the thornbush)
the coffin rising out of the ground
the old smelly magician himself no less
rising out of the coffin.

He gathers about him his mothy purple cloak.

Daft and drunk with spells
he smiles lopsidedly.
His feet munch on gravel.

He is coming he is coming here
(Hi brighteyes! Hiya brighteyes!)
he is waving that unconvincing
wand he bought in Woolworths.
He has dipped it in a luminous
low-grade oil pool.
Bored with his own act he shouts
JEHOVAH ONE BAAL NIL
Then a lightning flash ha ha
a bit of a rumble of thunder.
Nothing much you understand.
Why should the agèd peacock
stretch his wings?

At once the scientists take off
the priests hurry up
into the sky. They zoom.
They free-wheel high over rooftops
playing guitars;
they perform exquisite
figures of 8
but the old mediocre reprobate
merely shrinks them
then returns to his smelly coffin.
Slowly winking he pulls down the lid

slowly the coffin sinks into the ground.
(Bye brighteyes! Arrivederci brighteyes!)

I wave. I blink.
The thunder has cleared
the summer afternoon is vacated.
As if a cannon had been fired
doves and crows
circle the abandoned green lawns.

4   *The poetry reading*

Coughing and echo of echoes.
A lofty resonant public place.
It is the assembly hall.
Wooden chairs on wooden planks.
Suddenly he enters suddenly
a hush but for the small
distraction of one chair
squeaking in torment on a plank
then his voice unnatural.

He is an underground vatic poet.
His purple plastic coat is enchanting.
Indeed he is chanting
'Fu–er–uck Fu–er–uck'
with spiritual concentration.
Most of us laugh
because the others are laughing
most of us clap
because the others are clapping.

In the Interval out of focus
in the foyer Mr Poet signs his books.
My atheist uncle asseverates
that opus you read Fuck Fuck –
a most affecting and effective
social protest Mr Poet.

In the ladies' corner though
Marian eyeing the bard
maintains he is a real
sexual messiah
that his poem was not an expletive
but an incitement.
Fat Blondie cannot cease from crying.
She thinks his poem so nostalgic.

Meanwhile the superintendent asks
Mr Poet what is a poem?
The first words Eve spoke to Adam?
The last words Adam spoke to Eve
as they slouched from Paradise?

Mr Poet trembles
he whistles
he shakes his head Oi Oi.
As if his legs were under water
he lifts up and down in slow motion
up and down his heavy feet
he rubs the blood vessels in his eyes
he punches with a steady rhythm
his forehead

and then at last
there is the sound of gritty clockwork
the sound of a great whirring.

He is trying to say something.
His sputum is ostentatious
his voice comes through the long ago.

After the interval
the hall clatters raggedly into silence.
Somewhere else distant
a great black bell is beating
the sound of despair
and then is still.
Cu-er-unt Cu-er-unt chants the poet.
We applaud politely
wonder whether he is telling or asking.
The poet retires a trifle ill.
We can all see that he requires air.

5   *Visiting day*

The superintendent told us
that last summer on vacation
he saw a blind poet
reading Homer
on a Greek mountainside.

As a result my atheist uncle
has fitted black lenses
into his spectacles.

94

They are so opaque
he cannot see through them.
He walks around with a white stick.
We shout Copycat Copycat.

In reply his mouth utters
I don't want to see I can't bear to see
any more junk dropping down.
Meanwhile visitors of different sizes
in circumspect clothes in small groups
are departing from the great lawns –
though one alone lags behind and is waving.

She in that blue orgone dress waving
reminds me how I wrote a letter once.
'Love read this though it has little meaning
for by reading this you give me meaning'
I wrote or think I wrote or meant to write
and receiving no reply I heard
the silence.
Now I see a stranger waving.

October evenings are so moody.
A light has gone on
in the superintendent's office.
There are rumours that next week
all of us will be issued
with black specs.

Maybe yes maybe no.

But now the gates have closed
now under the huge unleafy trees
there is nobody.
Father father there is no-one.
We are only middle-aged.
There are too many ghosts already.
We remain behind like evergreens.

6   *Autumn in Funland*

These blue autumn days
we turn on the water taps.
Morse knockings in the pipes
dark pythagorean
interpretations.

The more we know
the more we journey into ignorance.

All day mysterious aeroplanes
fly over
leaving theurgic vapour trails
dishevelled by the wind
horizontal chalky lines
from some secret script
announcing names perhaps
of those about to die.

Downstairs the superintendent
sullen as a ruined millionaire

says nothing does nothing
stares through the dust-flecked window.
He will not dress a wound even.
He cannot stop a child from crying.

Again at night
shafting through the dark
on the bedroom walls
a veneer wash of radium
remarkably disguised
as simple moonlight.
My vertebral column
is turning into glass.

O remember
the atrocities of the Thracians.
They are deadly cunning.
Our water is polluted.
Our air is polluted.
Soon our orifices will bleed.

These black revolving nights
we are all funambulists.
The stars below us
the cerebellum disordered
we juggle on the edge of the earth
one foot on earth
one foot over the abyss.

With considerable poise
in a darkening room
the superintendent sat immobile
for hours at the polished table.
His heart had stopped in the silence
between two beats.

Down with the Thracians.
Down with the Thracians
who think God has blue hair and red eyes.
Down with the bastard Thracians
who somehow killed our superintendent.

Yesterday the morning of the funeral
as instructed by Pythagoras
all members on waking kept their eyes closed
all stared at the blackness
in the back of their eyelids
all heard far away five ancient sounds fading.

Today it's very cold.
Fat Blondie stands inconsolable
in the middle of the goldfish pool.
She will not budge.
The musky waters have amputated her feet.
Both her eyes are crying simultaneously.
She holds her shoes in her right hand
and cries and cries.

Meantime our American guest tries
the sophistry of a song.
The only happiness we know she sings
is the happiness that's gone
and Mr Poet moans like a cello
that's most itself when most melancholy.

To all of this
my atheist uncle responds magnificently.
In his funeral black specs
he will be our new leader.
Look how spitting on his hands first
he climbs the flagpole.
Wild at the very top he shouts
I AM IMMORTAL.

8   *Lots of snow*

First the skies losing height
then snow raging and the revolution bungled.
Afterwards in the silence
between two snowfalls
we deferred to our leader.
We are but shrubs not tall cedars.

Let Pythagoras be
an example to all Thracian spies
my tyrant uncle cried
retiring to the blackness inside
a fat Edwardian pillar box.
Who's next for the icepick?

Already the severed head of Pythagoras
transforms the flagpole
into a singularly
long white neck.

It has become a god that cannot see
how the sun drips its dilutions
on dumpy snowacres.

And I? I write a letter to someone nameless
in white ink on white paper
to an address unknown.
Oh love I write
surely love was no less
because less uttered or more accepted?

My bowels are made of glass.
The western skies try to rouge the snow.
I goosestep across this junk of heaven
to post my blank envelope.

Slowly night begins in the corner
where two walls meet.
The cold is on the crocus.
Snows mush and melt
and small lights fall from twigs.

Bright argus-eyed the thornbush.
Approaching the pillar box
I hear its slit of darkness screaming.

Uncle stood behind me
when I read Mr Poet's poster
on the billiard cloth
of the noticeboard:
COME TO THE THORNBUSH TONIGHT
HEAR THE VOICES ENTANGLED IN IT
MERLIN'S
MESMER'S
ALL THE UNSTABLE MAGICIANS
YEH YEH
DR BOMBASTUS TOO
FULL SUPPORTING CAST.

Not me I said thank you no
I'm a rational man touch wood.
Mesmer is dead these many years
and his purple cloak in rags.

They are all dead replied uncle
don't you know yet
        all of them dead –
gone where they don't play billiards
haven't you heard the news?

And Elijah the meths drinker
what about Elijah I asked
who used to lie on a parkbench
in bearded sleep – he too?

Of course sneered uncle
smashed smashed years ago like the rest of them
gone with the ravens gone with the lightning.
Why else each springtime
with the opening of a door
no-one's there?

Now at the midnight ritual
we invoke Elijah Merlin Mesmer the best of them
gone with the ravens gone with the lightning
as we stand as usual in concentric circles
around the thornbush.
Something will happen tonight.

Next to me fat Blondie sobs.
Latterly she is much given to sobbing.
The more she sobs the more she suffers.

Suddenly above us
frightful insane
the full moon breaks free from a cloud
stares both ways
and the stars in their stalls tremble.

It enters the black arena aghast
at being seen and by what it can see.
It hoses cold fire over the crowd
over the snowacres of descending
unending slopes.

At last in the distance we hear
the transmigration of souls
like clarinets untranquil played by ghosts
that some fools think to be the wind.

Fat Blondie stops her crying
tilts her face towards me amazed
and holds my hand as if I too were dying.
For a moment I feel as clean as snow.

Do not be misled I say
sometimes Funland can be beautiful
But she takes her hand away.

I can see right through her.
She has become luminous glass.
She is dreaming of the abyss.
We are all dreaming of the abyss
when we forget what we are dreaming of.

But now this so-called moonlight
is changing us all to glass.
We must disperse say goodbye.
We cannot see each other.

Goodbye Blondie goodbye uncle goodbye.

Footprints in the snow
resume slowly up the slope.

They gave me chewing gum so I chewed.

Who's next for the icepick?

Tell me are we ice or are we glass?

Ask Abaris who stroked my gold thigh.

Fu-er-uck fu-er-uck.

Do not wake us. We may die.

Watching a Cloud

A lacy mobile changing lazily
its animals, unstable faces, till
I imagine an angel, his vapours sailing
asleep at different speeds. My failing:

to see similes, cloud as something other.
Is all inspiration correspondences?

Machinery of cloud and angel both are silent,
both insubstantial. Neither violent.

And, truly, if one shining angel existed
what safer than the camouflage of a cloud?
There's deranged wind up there. God its power!
Let me believe in angels for an hour.

Let sunlight fade on walls and a huge blind
be drawn faster than a horse across this field.
I want to be theological, stare through
raw white angel-fabric at holy bits of blue.

Let long theatrical beams slant down
to stage-strike that hill into religion. Me too!
An angel drifts to the East, its edges burning;
sunny sunlight on stony stone returning.

The Weeping

After I lean from my shadow
to switch on the dark in the lamp,
I sense distant riders
and a disembodied crone-voice rasping,
'Do not weep like a woman
for what you would not fight for as a man.'

Eyes closed before sleep
I think how sleep is a going into exile;
how shadows also
are but cut-out pieces of darkness
exiled from darkness.
(Each summer's day especially,
the diaspora of shadows
awaits the return of night.)

Already, clearly, I hear the advance
of horses, their regular pounding.
Soon two shadows on horseback appear:
one Boabdil, a king long dead,
the other, his scolding mother.
What is dream, what is not dream?
They ride round the corner
of night. They loom near
and become substance. They halt
their horses. They look back
at the alhambra of fable.
(Years since I, a tourist, sauntered
in the alhambra of fable,
read their guidebook story.)

Not the most woeful sound a man may hear,
an exile weeping and weeping.
Yet desolate it is
like a ram's horn blown
in a hushed synagogue,
like Christian bells opening, closing,
like the muezzin heard

even after he has ceased.
Such is the sound this man makes
looking back with clarifying remorse.
No man weeping either,
but a silhouette of a man,
a hunched shadow on horseback,
a homeless shadow weeping.

      And I wake up
weeping. I and another both weep
in the darkness, weep in unison.
I wake up. I sit up and stop weeping.
      No-one weeps.

Florida

Not one poem about an animal, she said,
in five, six volumes of poetry,
not one about The Peaceable Kingdom.
An accusation. Was she from the RSPCA?
Your contemporaries have all composed
inspired elegies for expired beasts;
told of salmon flinging themselves up
the sheer waterfall; cold crows,
in black rags, loitering near motorways;
parables of foxes and pheasants,
owls and voles, mice and moles,

cats, bats, pigs, pugs, snails, quails;
so why can't you write one, just one *haiku*?
Oh, I said, Oh! – then wondered if she knew
the story of the starving dowager.

The lady looked as solemn as No.
Well, during the French Revolution,
the dowager, becoming thinner and thinner,
invited other lean aristocrats to dinner.
That night the guests saw (I continued)
slowly roasting on a rotating spit
the dowager's own poodle, Fido,
who proved to be most succulent.
So they made a feast of it.
Afterwards, the dowager sighed,
fingering the pearls about her neck,
sighed and said in noble French,
(I translate) What a damn shame Fido
isn't alive to eat up all those nice
crunchy bones left upon the plate.

My story over, I waited for applause. We'd
never cease from crying, she said,
if *one* insect could relate its misery.
Quite, I said, looking at my paws.
In Florida I saw a floating log
change and chase and swallow up
a barking dog. Hell, I said, an alligator?
A museum snake, too, in Gainesville,
Murder City, I can't forget,
poor black priapus in an empty case

lifting up its head for food not there.
With your gift I'd make a poem out of that.
So try, she said, do try and write
a creature poem and call it *Florida*.
I closed my eyes and she receded.

I thought of tigers and of Blake,
I thought of Fido and his bones.
No, no, she cried, think of Florida.
I saw the hotels of Miami Beach,
I heard waves collapsing ceaselessly.
No no, she said, think again, think
of Florida, its creature kingdom.
Like a TV screen my imagination
lit up to startle the ghost of Blake
with my own eidetic ads for Florida:
first, that black frustrated snake erect,
then two *grapefruit* inside a brassière.
Open your eyes, the lady screamed, *wake up*.
I'm a poor bifurcated animal, I apologized.
Eagle beagle, bug grub, boar bear.

Uncle Isidore

When I observe a toothless ex-violinist,
with more hair than face, sprawled like Karl Marx
on a park seat or slumped, dead or asleep,

in the central heat of a public library
I think of Uncle Isidore – smelly
schnorrer and lemon-tea bolshevik – my foreign
distant relative, not always distant.

Before Auschwitz, Treblinka, he seemed near,
those days of local pogroms, five year programmes,
until I heard him say, 'Master, Master
of the Universe, blessed be your name,
don't you know there's been no rain for years
and your people are thirsty? Have you no shame,
compassion? Don't you care at all?'

And fitting the violin to his beard
he bitterly asked me – no philosopher
but a mere boy – 'What difference between
the silence of God and the silence of men?'
Then, distant, as if in the land of Uz,
the answering sky let fall the beautiful
evening sound of thunder and of serious rain.

That was the first time Uncle went lame,
the first time the doctor came and quit hopelessly.
His right foot raised oddly to his left knee,
some notes wrong, all notes wild, unbalanced,
he played and he played not to that small child
who, big-eyed, listened – but to the Master
of the Universe, blessed be his name.

Tales of Shatz

Meet Rabbi Shatz in his correct black homburg.
The cheder boys call him Ginger.
If taller than 5 foot you're taller than him;
also taller than his father,
grandfather, great grandfather.

Meet Ruth Shatz, née Ruth Pinsky,
short-statured too, straight-backed.
In her stockinged feet
her forehead against his,
her eyes smile into his.
And again on the pillow, later.
Ah those sexy red-headed Pinskys
of Leeds and Warsaw: her mother,
grandmother, great grandmother!

Mrs Shatz resembles Rabbi Shatz's mother.
Rabbi Shatz resembles Mrs Shatz's father.
Strangers mistake them for brother, sister.

At University, Solly Shatz, their morning star,
suddenly secular, all 6 foot of him –
a black-haired centre-forward on Saturdays –
switches studies from Theology to Genetics.

★

A certain matron of Golders Green,
fingering amber beads about her neck,
approaches Rabbi Shatz.
When I was a small child, she thrills,

once, just once, God the Holy One
came through the curtains of my bedroom.
What on earth has he been doing since?

Rabbi Shatz turns, he squints,
he stands on one leg
hoping for the inspiration of a Hillel.
The Holy One, he answers, blessed be He,
has been waiting, waiting patiently,
till you see Him again.

★

Consider the mazzle of Baruch Levy
who changed his name to Barry Lee,
who moved to Esher, Surrey,
who sent his four sons – Matthew, Mark,
Luke and John – to boarding school,
who had his wife's nose fixed,
who, blinking in the Gents,
turned from the writing on the wall
and later, still blinking, joined the golf club.

With new friend, Colonel Owen,
first game out, under vexed clouds,
thunder detonated without rain,
lightning stretched without thunder,
and near the 2nd hole,
where the darker green edged
to the shaved lighter green,
both looked up terrified.

Barbed fire zagged towards them
to strike dead instantly
Mostyn Owen, Barry Lee's opponent.
What luck that Colonel Owen
(as Barry discovered later)
once was known as Moshe Cohen.

Now, continued Rabbi Shatz,
recall how even the sorrows of Job
had a happy ending.

★

Being a religious man Shatz adored riddles.
Who? he asked his impatient wife.

Who like all men came into this world
with little fists closed, departed
with large hands open, yet on walking
over snow and away from sunsets
followed no shadow in front of him,
left no footprint behind him?

You don't know either, opined his wife.
You and your Who? Who?
Are you an owl?
Why do you always pester me with riddles
you don't know the answer of?

Rabbi Shatz for some reason wanted to cry.
If I knew the answers, he whispered,

would my questions still be riddles?
And he tiptoed away, closed the door
so softly behind him
as if on a sleeping dormitory.

Often when listening to music
before a beautiful slow movement
recaptured him, Shatz would blank out,
hear nothing. So now, too, in his lit study
as night rain tilted outside
across dustbins in the lane
he forgot why his lips moved, his body swayed.

Cousin Sidney

Dull as a bat, said my mother
of cousin Sidney in 1940 that time he tried
to break his garden swing, jumping on it,
size 12 shoes – at fifteen the tallest boy
in the class, taller than loping Dan Morgan
when Dan Morgan wore his father's top hat.

Duller than a bat, said my father
when hero Sidney lied about his age
to claim rough khaki, silly ass;
and soon, somewhere near Dunkirk,

some foreign corner was forever Sidney
though uncle would not believe it.

Missing not dead please God, please,
he said, and never bolted the front door,
never string taken from the letter box,
never the hall light off lest his one son
came home through a night of sleet
whistling, We'll meet again.

Aunt crying and raw in the onion air
of the garden (the unswinging empty swing)
her words on a stretched leash
while uncle shouted, Bloody Germans.
And on November 11th, two howls
of silence even after three decades

till last year, their last year,
when uncle and aunt also went missing,
missing alas, so that now strangers
have bolted their door and cut the string
and no-one at all (the hall so dark)
waits up for Sidney, silly ass.

Remembrance Day

Unbuttoned at home, last Sunday afternoon,
Violence snored in the armchair.
This week, eyes moist, our neighbour marches
with the veterans, ready to be televised,
his nationalism narrow as the coffin
in which the invented hero lies.

A vision dies from being too long stared at.
Not only songs of the old wars fade but ghosts
on barbed wire, on a bayonet-blade. Yet still
everything is what it is and another thing
as the black-coated ceremonies begin
under a vapour trail in blue cold skies.

2000 men are taking off their hats. Not one cries
'Folly'; not one from somewhere else
when the hollow trumpets toot and the guns
damply thud. Echo of an echo of an echo
vanishing like that vapour trail.
Whatever happened to you, Dolly?

By nightfall, smoke lurks down pub-lit streets
and cheers! cheers! mademoiselle from 'Armentières';
and did you die of cancer, Lily Marlene?
You have forgotten, cannot touch the pinewood.
So Violence, beery, lonely as an old tune,
lifts his lapel to smell the paper poppy.

Sons

Sarcastic sons slam front doors.
So a far door slams and I think
of Cardiff outskirts where, once, captured acres played
at being small tamed gardens: the concrete way
roads supplanted grass, wild flowers, bosky paths.
Now my son is like that, altering every day.

I was like that; also like
those new semis that seemed ashamed,
their naked windows slashed across by whitewash.
At the frontier of Nowhere order and chaos clash.
And who's not lived at the frontier of Nowhere
and being adolescent was both prim and brash?

Strange a London door should slam
and I think thus, of Cardiff evenings
trying to rain, of quick dark where raw brick could hide,
could dream of being ruins where ghosts abide.
Do spreading lamps assert themselves too early?
Anglo-Welsh home town, half town half countryside.

Son, you are like that and I
love you for it. In adult rooms
the hesitant sense of not belonging quite.
Too soon maturity will civilize your night,
thrust down electric roots, the nameless becoming
consolingly named and your savage darkness bright.

The Stethoscope

Through it,
over young women's tense abdomens,
I have heard the sound of creation
and, in a dead man's chest, the silence
    before creation began.

Should I
pray therefore? Hold this instrument in awe
and aloft a procession of banners?
Hang this thing in the interior
    of a cold, mushroom-dark church?

Should I
kneel before it, chant an apophthegm
from a small text? Mimic priest or rabbi,
the swaying noises of religious men?
    Never! Yet I could praise it.

I should
by doing so celebrate my own ears,
by praising them praise speech at midnight
when men become philosophers;
    laughter of the sane and insane;

night cries
of injured creatures, wide-eyed or blind;
moonlight sonatas on a needle;
lovers with doves in their throats; the wind
    travelling from where it began.

White Coat, Purple Coat

White coat and purple coat
   a sleeve from both he sews.
That white is always stained with blood,
   that purple by the rose.

And phantom rose and blood most real
   compose a hybrid style;
white coat and purple coat
   few men can reconcile.

White coat and purple coat
   can each be worn in turn
but in the white a man will freeze
   and in the purple burn.

A Touch of Snow

(Joan's)

Now that the evening cold is on the crocus
do you feel the ache of something missing?
Snow melts falling, a million small lights fuse

on twigs, fall to pools of darkness on the ground
while, indoors, one note's gone from the piano
– the highest. Listen to the thud of felt.

No, dear, no! Hear rather the other notes
of the right hand. Also the left background.
Their rejoicing, lamenting, candid sound.

Bedtime Story

Adam, the first man, my father said, perfect
like the letter A. Blessed be all alephs.
Then my clever question: were there no creatures,

father, before Adam? A long index finger
vertical as a flame to horizontal lips.
Eyes right, eyes left. Whisper of a spy:

yes, unfortunate creatures, angels botched,
badly made, born to be vagrant, born with
the usual amnesia but with little sense

and no sense of direction. They could not
deliver the simplest of messages . . .
Now, late, I think of that flawed lineage:

of one announcing great news to the wrong Mary
– perhaps it was that unshaved derelict
at the bus station with an empty bottle, muttering –

and here's another in disguise, down at heel,
defeated face white as the salt of Sodom,
veteran among the homeward football crowd

shuffling under hoardings towards nightfall;
and this one supine, over-bearded,
sleeping on a parkbench in his excrement.

Dogs bark and bark at them. They lack pleasure.
They refrigerate the coldness of things.
They stale. They taste the age of their own mouths.

In Casualty rarely cry or grumble.
In wards die with only screens around them.
But now, father, here's *my* bedtime story:

sometimes in the last light of January,
in treeless districts of cities, in a withered
backstreet, their leader can be glimpsed from trains.

He stands motionless in long black overcoat
on spoilt snow and seems like a man again
who yet, father, will outlast the letter Z.

In the Gallery

Outside it is snow snow
but here, under the chandelier,
there's no such thing as weather.
Right wall, a horse (not by Géricault);
left, a still life, mainly apples;
between, on the parquet floor, a box
or a coffin which is being opened.

Through a gold-framed mirror
the Director, dressed as if for mourning,
observes the bust
of an unknown lady
by an unknown sculptor
being lifted out of the straw
by a man in overalls.

2

The apples do not rot, the horse will not bolt,
the statue of the lady
cannot breathe one spot
of tissue paper on the mirror.

Her name is forgotten,
the sculptor's name is disputed,
they both have disappeared forever.
They could have been born
in the North or the South.
They have no grave anywhere.

3

Outside it is snow snow
snowing and namelessness is growing.

Yesterday four hoofmarks in the snows
rose and flew away.

They must have been four crows.
Or, maybe, three of them were crows.

A Winter Visit

Now she's ninety I walk through the local park
where, too cold, the usual peacocks do not screech
and neighbouring lights come on before it's dark.

Dare I affirm to her, so aged and so frail,
that from one pale dot of peacock's sperm
spring forth all the colours of a peacock's tail?

I do. But she like the sibyl says, 'I would die';
then complains, 'This winter I'm half dead, son.'
And because it's true I want to cry.

Yet must not (although only Nothing keeps)
for I inhabit a white coat not a black
even here – and am not qualified to weep.

So I speak of small approximate things,
of how I saw, in the park, four flamingoes
standing, one-leggèd on ice, heads beneath wings.

The Doctor

Guilty, he does not always like his patients.
But here, black fur raised, their yellow-eyed dog
mimics Cerberus, barks barks at the invisible,
so this man's politics, how he may crawl
to superiors, do not matter. A doctor must care
and the wife's on her knees in useless prayer,
the young daughter's like a waterfall.

Quiet, Cerberus! Soon enough you'll have a bone
or two. Now, coughing, the patient expects
the unjudged lie: 'Your symptoms are familiar
and benign' – someone to be cheerfully sure,
to transform tremblings, gigantic unease,
by naming like a pet some small disease
with a known aetiology, certain cure.

So the doctor will and yes he will prescribe
the usual dew from a banana leaf; poppies and
honey too; ten snowflakes or something whiter
from the bole of a tree; the clearest water
ever, melting ice from a mountain lake;
sunlight from waterfall's edge, rainbow smoke;
tears from eyelashes of the daughter.

X-ray

Some prowl sea-beds, some hurtle to a star
and, mother, some obsessed turn over every stone
or open graves to let that starlight in.
There are men who would open anything.

Harvey, the circulation of the blood,
and Freud, the circulation of our dreams,
pried honourably and honoured are
like all explorers. Men who'd open men.

And those others, mother, with diseases
like great streets named after them: Addison,
Parkinson, Hodgkin — physicians who'd arrive
fast and first on any sour death-bed scene.

I am their slowcoach colleague, half afraid,
incurious. As a boy it was so: you know how

my small hand never teased to pieces
an alarm clock or flensed a perished mouse.

And this larger hand's the same. It stretches now
out from a white sleeve to hold up, mother,
your X-ray to the glowing screen. My eyes look
but don't want to; I still don't want to know.

Lunch with a Pathologist

My colleague knows by heart the morbid verse
of facts – the dead weight of a man's liver,
a woman's lungs, a baby's kidneys.

At lunch he recited unforgettably,
'After death, of all soft tissues the brain's
the first to vanish, the uterus the last.'

'Yes,' I said, 'at dawn I've seen silhouettes
hunched in a field against the skyline, each one
feasting, preoccupied, silent as gas.

Partial to women they've stripped women bare
and left behind only the taboo food,
the uterus, inside the skeleton.'

My colleague wiped his mouth with a napkin,
hummed, picked shredded meat from his canines,
said, 'You're a peculiar fellow, Abse.'

Pantomime Diseases

When the fat Prince french-kissed Sleeping Beauty
her eyelids opened wide. She heard applause,
the photographer's shout, wedding-guest laughter.
Poor girl – she married the Prince out of duty
and suffered insomnia ever after.

The lies of Once-upon-a-Time appal.
Cinderella seeing white mice grow into horses
shrank to the wall – an event so ominous
she didn't go to the Armed Forces Ball
but phoned up Alcoholics Anonymous.

Snow White suffered from profound anaemia.
The genie warned, 'Aladdin, you'll go blind,'
when that little lad gleefully rubbed his lamp.
The Babes in the Wood died of pneumonia.
D. Whittington turned back because of cramp.

Shy, in the surgery, Red Riding Hood undressed
– Dr Wolff, the fool, diagnosed Scarlet Fever.
That Jill who tumbled down has wrecked her back,

that Puss-in-Boots has gout and is depressed
and one bare bear gave Goldilocks a heart attack.

When the three Darling children thought they'd fly
to Never-Never Land – the usual trip –
their pinpoint pupils betrayed addiction.
And not hooked by Captain Hook but by
that ponce, Peter Pan! All the rest is fiction.

Snake

When the snake bit
Rabbi Hanina ben Dosa
while he was praying

the snake died. (Each day
is attended by surprises
or it is nothing.)

Question: was the bare-footed,
smelly Rabbi more poisonous
than the snake

or so God-adulterated
he'd become immune
to serpent poison?

Oh great-great-great-uncles,
your palms weighing air,
why are you arguing?

Listen, the snake thought
(being old and unwell
and bad-tempered as hell)

Death, where's thy sting?
In short, was just testing:
a snake's last fling.

Yes, the *so-called* snake
was dying anyway, its heart
calcified and as old as Eden.

No, that snake was A1 fit
but while hissing for fun it
clumsily bit its own tongue.

No, Hanina invented that snake;
not for his own sake but for first-
class, religious publicity.

No no, here's the key to it.
Ask: did the Rabbi, later on,
become a jumpy, timid man?

Remember, he who has been bitten
by a snake thereafter becomes
frightened of a rope . . .

Bearded men in darkening rooms
sipping lemon tea and arguing
about the serpent till the moon

of Russia, of Latvia, Lithuania,
Poland, rose above the alien
steeples – centuries of sleep.

Now, tonight, a clean-shaven rabbi
who once studied in Vienna
says snake-venom contains

haemolysins, haemo-
coagulants, protolysins,
cytolysins and neurotoxins

and that even in Hanina
ben Dosa's day a snake was a
snake – unless, of course, it was

a penis, an unruly penis,
making a noise like one pissing
on a mound of fresh hot ashes.

Oh great-great-great-uncles
did you hear him? And are your
handbones weighing moonshine?

Of Itzig and His Dog

To pray for the impossible,
says Itzig, is disgraceful.
I prefer, when I'm on my own,
when I'm only with my dog,
when I can't go out
because of the weather,
because of my shoes,
to talk very intimately to God.

    Itzig, they nag, why do that,
   what's the point of that?
   God never replies surely?

Such ignorance! Am I at the Western Wall?
Am I on spacious Mount Sinai?
Is there a thornbush in this murky room?
God may never say a word,
may never even whisper, Itzig, hullo.

But when I'm talking away
to the right and to the left,
when it's raining outside,
when there's rain on the glass,
when I say please God this
and thank God that,
then God always makes, believe me,
the dog's tail wag.

Street Scene

(Outside the grocer's, Golders Green Road)

They quarrel, this black–bearded man
and his busy, almost flying wife –
she with her hands, he with proverbs.

'He who never rebukes his son,'
says the bearded man too blandly,
'leads him into delinquency.'

And she who hasn't studied nicely
such studied wisdom, now replies,
'You're a, you're a, you're a donkey.'

Three or four psychiatrists smile
as they pass the greengrocer's shop.
Again, patient, he quotes the Talmud:

'When one suggests you're a donkey
do not fret; only when two speak thus
go buy yourself a saddle.'

But she has thrown appropriate
carrots carrots at his sober head
and one sticks brightly in his beard.

Truce! You have been led into fiction.
Listen! Here comes a violin
and tunes to make a donkey dance.

The bearded man has closed his eyes.
Who's this, disguised as a beggar,
playing a violin without strings?

What music's this, its cold measure?
Who are these, dangling from lamp-posts,
kicking as if under water?

A Note to Donald Davie in Tennessee

Wigged gluttony never your style but will you
                always eschew,
barbered, the anorexia of fanaticism?
Though we would seldom sign the same petition
or join awkwardly the same shouting march,
neither of us, I hope, would leave through those doors
on the right or on the left marked HYGIENE.

Donald, you're such a northern-rooted man
                you've moved again.
Is home only home away from it? Still poets
jog eagerly, each molehill mistaken
for Parnassus – such energy articulate!
But where's the avant-garde when the procession
runs continuously in a closed circle?

So many open questions to one who prefers
                fugitive ways.
Of course I salute your gifted contradictions –
your two profiles almost the same – like Martin Guerre's.
I too am a reluctant puritan, feel uneasy
sometimes as if I travelled without ticket.
Yet here I am in England way out in the centre.

A Sea-Shell for Vernon Watkins

A stage moon and you, too, unreal, unearthed.
Then two shadows athletic down the cliffs
of Pennard near the nightshift of the sea.
You spoke of Yeats and Dylan, your sonorous
pin-ups. I thought, *relentless romantic!*
Darkness stayed in a cave and I lifted
a sea-shell from your shadow when you big-talked
how the dead resume the silence of God.

The bank calls in its debts and all are earthed.
Only one shadow at Pennard today
and listening to another sea-shell I found,
startled, its phantom sea utterly silent –
the shell's cochlea scooped out. Yet appropriate
that small void, that interruption of sound,
for what should be heard in a shell at Pennard
but the stopped breath of a poet who once sang loud?

Others gone also, like you dispensable,
famed names once writ in gold on spines of books
now rarely opened, the young asking, 'Who?'
The beaches of the world should be strewn with such
dumb shells while the immortal sea syllables
in self-love its own name, 'Sea, Sea, Sea, Sea.'
I turn to leave Pennard. This shell is useless.
If I could cry I would but not for you.

Imitations

In this house, in this afternoon room,
my son and I. The other side of glass
snowflakes whitewash the shed roof and the grass
this surprised April. My son is sixteen,
an approximate man. He is my chameleon,
my soft diamond, my deciduous evergreen.

Eyes half closed he listens to pop forgeries
of music – how hard it is to know – and perhaps
dreams of some school Juliet I don't know.
Meanwhile, beyond the bending window,
gusting suddenly, despite a sky half blue,
a blur of white blossom, whiter snow.

And I stare, oh immortal springtime, till
I'm elsewhere and the age my cool son is,

my father alive again (I, his duplicate),
his high breath, my low breath, sticking to the glass
while two white butterflies stumble, held each
to each as if by elastic, and pass.

In My Fashion

Dear, they said that woman resembled you.
Was that why I went with her, flirted with her,
raised my right hand to her left breast
till I heard the still sad music of humanity?
I complimented you! Why do you object?

Still you shrill, discover everything untrue:
your doppelgänger does not own your birthmarks,
cannot know our blurred nights together.
That music was cheap – a tune on a comb at best,
harsh and grating. Yes, you chasten me

and subdue. Well, that woman was contraband
and compared with you mere counterfeit.
Snow on the apple tree is not apple blossom –
all her colours wrong, approximate,
as in a reproduction of a masterpiece.

Last Words

Splendidly, Shakespeare's heroes,
Shakespeare's heroines, once the spotlight's on,
enact every night, with such grace, their verbose deaths.
Then great plush curtains, then smiling resurrection
to applause – and never their good looks gone.

The last recorded words too
of real kings, real queens, all the famous dead,
are but pithy pretences, quotable fictions
composed by anonymous men decades later,
never with ready notebooks at the bed.

Most do not know who they are
when they die or where they are, country or town,
nor which hand on their brow. Some clapped-out actor may
imagine distant clapping, bow, but no real queen
will sigh, 'Give me my robe, put on my crown.'

Death scenes not life-enhancing,
death scenes not beautiful nor with breeding;
yet bravo Sydney Carton, bravo Duc de Chavost
who, euphoric beside the guillotine, turned down
the corner of the page he was reading.

And how would I wish to go?
Not as in opera – that would offend –
nor like a blue-eyed cowboy shot and short of words,
but finger-tapping still our private morse, '. . . love you,'
before the last flowers and flies descend.

Phew!

Do you know that Sumerian proverb
'A man's wife is his destiny'?
But supposing you'd been here,
this most strange of meeting places,
5000 years too early? Or me,
a fraction of a century too late?
No angel with SF wings
would have beckoned,
'This way, madam, this way, sir.'

Have you ever, at a beach,
aimed one small pebble
at another, thrown high, higher?

And though what ends
happily
is never the end,
and though the secret is
there's another secret always,

because this, because that,
because on high the Blessèd
were playing ring-a-ring-o'-roses,
because millions of miles below,
during the Rasoumovsky,
the cellist, pizzicati,
played a comic, wrong note,
you looked to the right, luckily,
I looked to the left, luckily.

Horse

You can't quite
identify it
the long straight road
unsignposted
zipping between hedges
to a scandalously
gorgeous sunset.
As you look closer
shading your eyes
with your right hand
vigilant you'll see
the visitant
the white horse
halfway down it.

Do you remember?
Your father drove the car
the family squabbling
this way years ago
many a time
this Roman road
that's empty now
but for the distant
truant pink horse
with a barely
visible
red shadow
racing towards
the signals of sunset.

War-high in the sky
vapour trails fatten
and you know again
the common sense
of *déjà vu*. Perhaps
someone far from home
should be playing
a mouth organ
a melody slow
and sad and wanton
a tune you've heard
but can't quite say
as the purple horse
surprises the sunset.

And you close your eyes
trying to name it all.
But you recall only
the day's small prose
certain queachy things
what the office said
what the office did
as the sunset goes
as the black horse goes
into the darkness.
And you forget
how from the skin
below your thumbnail
your own moon rises.

In the Holiday Inn

After the party I returned to the hotel.
The room was too hot so I took off my coat.

It was January but I turned down the thermostat.
I took off my shirt but I was still too hot.

I opened the window, it was snowing outside.
Despite all this the air began to simmer.

The room had a pyrexia of unknown origin.
I took off my trousers, I took off my shorts.

This room was a cauldron, this room was tropical.
On the wall, the picture of willows changed

to palm trees. In the mirror I could see the desert.
I stood naked in my socks and juggled

with pomegranates. I offered offerings
that soon became burnt. This was some holiday.

I took off one sock and read the bible.
They were cremating idols, sacrificing oxen.

I could feel the heat of their fiery furnace.
I could hear those pyromaniacs chanting.

I could smell the singed wings of cherubim.
I took off the other sock and began to dance.

Like sand the carpet scalded my twinkling feet.
Steam was coming out of both my ears.

I was King David dancing before the Lord.
Outside it was snowing but inside it was Israel.

I danced six cubits this way, six cubits that.
Now at dawn I'm hotter than the spices of Sheba.

What shall I do? I shall ask my wise son,
Solomon. Where are you Solomon?

You are not yet born, you do not know
how wise you are or that I'm your father

and that I'm dancing and dancing.

Crepuscolo

Crepuscolo *is one of the partly finished
statues by Michelangelo in the Medici
Chapel, San Lorenzo.*

To the grey Sacristy of San Lorenzo
tourists come whispering lest they waken
this self-absorbed statue and it assail
each prying one of them, lest a stone hand

uplift to point and the stone head utter,
slowly turning, 'Wrongdoing and shame prevail!'

Once all drowsy in Carrara. Harmlessly,
unnumbered shadows brooded under the weight
of rock-ledges, lizards hardly animate.
Then certain men came. Still the stone's cry
safe and soundless, still the statue slumbered
in the refuge of the rock's estate.

But, soon, massive slabs were brutally urged
from the mountain – the half-bright, half-stripped bodies
of workmen struggling in dazzle and bone-
white powder of marble, smoking sunlight.
How could they discern the one waking there
or hear stone words in the larynx of the stone?

And later, in Florence? Only the sculptor
heard the statue, almost delivered, crying
'Dear to me is sleep, dearer to be at peace,
in stone, while wrongdoing and shame prevail.
Not to see, not to know, would be a great blessing.'
So the statue pleaded, so the sculptor ceased.

More than four hundred years since they set out
from Carrara, each mile cursed and supervised.
The body in the rock staying young but the hair
turning grey and the face ageing utterly –
its idioplasm fixed, its night-accepting look
despairingly defined in the eyes not there.

Now, this evening, on exercise, three warplanes
dive on Carrara, flee, return, rehearse
radioactive speeds so shamelessly
that, in the x-rayed mountain, another
fifty million statues cower, unhatched,
and not one, stone-enslaved, wanting to be free.

Case History

'Most Welshmen are worthless,
an inferior breed, doctor.'
He did not know I was Welsh.
Then he praised the architects
of the German death-camps –
did not know I was a Jew.
He called liberals, 'White blacks',
and continued to invent curses.

When I palpated his liver
I felt the soft liver of Goering;
when I lifted my stethoscope
I heard the heartbeats of Himmler;
when I read his encephalograph
I thought, 'Sieg heil, mein Führer.'

In the clinic's dispensary
red berry of black bryony,

cowbane, deadly nightshade, deathcap.
Yet I prescribed for him
as if he were my brother.

Later that night I must have slept
on my arm: momentarily
my right hand lost its cunning.

A Salute on the Way

(*To Peter Porter*)

In the Land of late Evening,
miles yet from the bus terminus
where the electric outskirts end
abruptly (far beyond, the Old
Management is about to mend
   the fused stars) I hear you laugh.
   A warm, democratic laugh.

But I remember your 'Alas'
when the needle played the 'sssh' of black
round and round the record's label.
Then the god's thesmothete decreed
(all his aces on the table)
   the game was over – your bill
   the cost of seriousness.

It seems you've often played the lead
in a tragedy translated
by a too cheerful Australian
where the hero, at home, bereaved,
alone and feeling alien,
    takes off unscripted glasses
    quietly, to rub his eyes.

Thus, in the Land of late Evening,
though I hear, now, your candid laugh
more generous than a bridegroom's,
I can guess how, afterwards, you,
like good St Peter, will resume
    the slightly-pained look of one
    about to be crucified

upside-down. Peter-come-lately,
it's your turn to complain of
a *Collected Poems*; of rust
in the morning pelvis; of teeth
touching; of colleagues become dust;
    and nothing to say except
    facts, cats, and thriving heartache,

or who pushed whom and which one fell
(that yellow stain *is* Humpty Dumpty)
so to hell with the Old Management's
jackal-headed, hired psychopomp
whispering of money unspent,
    out there, in the banked darkness:
    'Follow me, follow, follow.'

Friend, let's not hurry. Who believes
these days in a second edition?
May we, unremaindered, go slow,
shadows lengthening between lamp posts
on leafy pavements, or on snow,
    to the very last lamp post
    in the Land of late Evening.

A Translation from the Martian

    Who for the first time on earth saw the object
that earth-men call an and-mirror (sic)
    who incognito picked it up who stared at it whose
eyes widened whose sixth toe curled up
    who cried out delightedly
    'Father. Father.'

    Who hid it in his pocket who concealed the object
where his long-dead father lived
    who occasionally gazed at it
    who smiled at it sweetly who spoke to it softly
    'Father. Father.'

    Who returned home with it who kept his hand
upon his pocket who did not show the ghost to his wife
    who became suspicious who came close to smell
him who waited for his sixth toe to fall asleep who stole

the object from his pocket who secretly stared at
it who cried out scornfully
   'Ach. It's only an old woman.'

   Who took it to the window who watched it fall in
slow-motion who heard it clatter an hour later
on the red-hard rocks below
   where the and-mirror (sic) broke into moonlight.

Pathetic Fallacies

Afternoon Mirror

So vain that mirror on the wall.
It waits there and waits there
just to be looked at.

Evening Mirror

Lonely, wishes another mirror
could be brought in, close by, opposite,
that it may reproduce itself.

Morning Mirror

At last, at last, Visiting Hour.
My portrait gallery is open.
The Director does not seem pleased.

Encounter at a Greyhound Bus Station

If belief, like heaven, lies beyond the facts
what serpent flies with an ant between its teeth?

asked the over-bearded man with closed eyes.
Who are they who descend when they ascend?

this kabbalist with eyes closed, asked,
Are all men in disguise except those crying?

And what exists in a tree that doesn't exist,
its eggs looted by creatures not yet created?

★

Partial to paradoxes, disliking riddles,
I hummed and I hawed, I advocated

the secrets of lucidity. Then said,
Some talk in their sleep, very few sing.

Abruptly, the unwashed one opened his lids,
rattled one coin inside a tin.

I looked into the splendour of his eyes
and laid my hand upon my mouth.

★

Then he scoffed: You are like the deaf man
who knows nothing of music or of dance

yet blurts out, observing musicians play
and dancers dance – Stupid, how stupid

those who carve the air this way and that,
who blow out their cheeks and make them fat,

who mill about, clutch and maul each other
as if the very earth and all would fall.

★

And what could I, secular, say to that?
That I'm deaf to God but not in combat?

Cool pretensions of reason he'd dismiss
and if I threw stones he'd build a house.

Yet I begged: Dare to reveal, sir, not conceal;
not all, translucent, lose authority.

Fool, he replied, I'm empty, feed my tin,
which I did, of course, when the bus came in.

Exit

As my colleague prepares the syringe
(the drip flees its hour glass)

I feel the depression of Saul,
my mother's right hand grasping still,
her left hand suspiciously still,
and think – Shadow on the wall,
Nothing on the floor – of your
random, katabolic ways:

merciful sometimes, precise, but often
wild as delirium, or like a surgeon
with cataracts grievously unkind
as you are now, as you visit
this old lady – one beloved by me –
as you blunder and exit, moth-blind,
mistaking even the light
on mirrors for open windows;

and as my colleague prepares the syringe
I remember another butchering –
a botched suicide in a circumspect
bed-sitting room, a barely
discernible fake of a girl-corpse,
a marmoreal stillness perfect
except for the closed
plum-skin eyelids trembling;

and as my colleague prepares the syringe
I picture also a victim of war
near a road, a peasant left for dead,
conscious, black-tongued, long-agonized,
able to lift, as my mother can now,
at intervals, her troubled head.

And as my colleague drives the needle in
I want to know the meaning of this:

why the dark thalamus finally
can't be shut down when we sleep
with swift economy? Of that king
and his queen – David and Bathsheba –
the old parable is plain:
out of so much suffering
came forth the other child,
the wise child, the Solomon;

but what will spring from this
unredeemed, needless degradation,
this concentration camp for one?
My colleague forces the plunger down,
squeezes the temgesic out,
the fluid that will numb and stun.
'Shadow on the wall . . .' I call, 'Nothing
on the floor . . . Patron of the Arts!'

And as my colleague extracts the needle
from her vein, the temgesic acts
till the bruised exit's negotiated.
Then how victoriously
you hold the left passive hand
of the dummy in the bed
while I continue uselessly
to hold the other.

Apology

I have spoken so much lately
of death and of treachery,
better to have sung the forgotten
other song of Solomon.
Forgive me. I do not believe
the rainbow was invisible
till Noah saw it;
nor was I refreshed
by strange bread in the desert,
spring water in the desert.

The two drab tablets of stone
were two drab tablets of stone,
yet, beloved, this is my heritage;
also music of Solomon's song
on psaltery and dulcimer,
that which is lost but not lost –
like the beautiful rod of Aaron,
the beautiful rod of Aaron
first with its blossom
then with its ripe almonds.

A Wall

in a field in the County of Glamorgan.
You won't find it named in any guidebook.
It lies, plonk, in the middle of rising ground,

forty-four paces long, high as your eyes,
it begins for no reason, ends no place.
No other walls are adjacent to it.
Seemingly unremarkable, it's just there,
stones of different sizes, different greys.

Don't say this wall is useless, that the grass
on the shadow side is much like the other.
It exists for golden lichens to settle,
for butterflies in their obstacle race
chasing each other to the winning post,
for huddling sheep in a slanting rainfall,
for you to say, 'This wall is beautiful.'

The Origin of Music

When I was a medical student
I stole two femurs of a baby
from The Pathology Specimen Room.
Now I keep them in my pocket,
the right femur and the left femur.
Like a boy scout, I'm prepared.
For what can one say to a neighbour
when his wife dies? 'Sorry'?
Or when a friend's sweet child
suffers leukaemia? 'Condolences'?

No, if I should meet either friend
or stricken neighbour in the street
and he should tell me, whisper to me,
his woeful, intimate news,
wordless I take the two small femurs
from out of my pocket sadly
and play them like castanets.

Carnal Knowledge

I

You, student, whistling those elusive bits
of Schubert when phut, phut, phut, throbbed the sky
of London. Listen: the servo-engine cut
and the silence was not the desired silence
between two movements of music. Then
Finale, the Aldwych echo of crunch
and the urgent ambulances loaded
with the fresh dead. You, young, whistled again,
entered King's, climbed the stone-murky steps
to the high and brilliant Dissecting Room
where nameless others, naked on the slabs,
reclined in disgraceful silences – twenty
amazing sculptures waiting to be vandalized.

2

You, corpse, I pried into your bloodless meat
without the morbid curiosity of Vesalius,
did not care that the great Galen was wrong,
Avicenna mistaken, that they had described
the approximate structure of pigs and monkeys
rather than the human body. With scalpel
I dug deep into your stale formaldehyde
unaware of Pope Boniface's decree
but, as instructed, violated you –
the reek of you in my eyes, my nostrils,
clothes, in the kisses of my girlfriends.
You, anonymous. Who were you, mister?
Your thin mouth could not reply, 'Absent, sir,'
or utter with inquisitionary rage.

    Your neck exposed, muscles, nerves, vessels,
a mere coloured plate in some anatomy book;
your right hand, too, dissected, never belonged,
it seemed, to somebody once shockingly alive,
never held, surely, another hand in greeting
or tenderness, never clenched a fist in anger,
never took up a pen to sign an authentic name.

    You, dead man, Thing, each day, each week,
each month, you, slowly decreasing Thing,
visibly losing Divine proportions,
you residue, mere trunk of a man's body,
you, X, legless, armless, headless Thing
that I dissected so casually.

    Then went downstairs to drink wartime coffee.

3

When the hospital priest, Father Jerome,
remarked, 'The Devil made the lower parts
of a man's body, God the upper,'
I said, 'Father, it's the other way round.'
So, the anatomy course over, Jerome,
thanatologist, did not invite me
to the Special Service for the Twenty Dead –
did not say to me, 'Come for the relatives' sake.'
(Surprise, surprise, that they had relatives,
those lifeless-size, innominate creatures.)
Other students accepted, joined in the fake chanting,
organ solemnity, cobwebbed theatre.
And that's all it would have been,
a ceremony propitious and routine,
an obligation forgotten soon enough
had not the strict priest with premeditated rage
called out the Register of the Twenty Dead –
each non-cephalic carcass gloatingly identified
with a local habitation and a name
till one by one, made culpable, the students cried.

4

I did not learn the name of my intimate,
the twentieth sculpture, the one next to the door.
No matter. Now all these years later
I know those twenty sculptures were but one,
the same one duplicated. You.
I hear not Father Jerome but St Jerome cry,
'No, John will be John, Mary will be Mary,'

as if the dead would have ears to hear
the Register on Judgement Day.
    Look, on gravestones many names.
There should be one only. Yours.
No, not even one since you have no name.
In the newspapers' memorial columns
many names. A joke.
On the canvases of masterpieces
the same figure always in disguise. Yours.
Even in the portraits of the old anchorite
fingering a dry skull you are half concealed
lest onlookers should turn away blinded.
In certain music, too, with its sound of loss,
in that Schubert Quintet, for instance,
you are there in the Adagio,
playing the third cello that cannot be heard.
    You are there and there and there, nameless,
and here I am, older by far and nearer,
perplexed, trying to recall what you looked like
before I dissected your face – you, threat,
molesting presence, and I in a white coat
your enemy, in a purple one, your nuncio,
writing this while a winter twig, not you,
scrapes, scrapes the windowpane.
    Soon I shall climb the stairs. Gratefully,
I shall wind up the usual clock at bedtime
(the steam vanishing from the bathroom mirror)
with my hand, my living hand.

A Prescription

Sweet-tempered, pestering
young man of Oxford
juggling with ghazals,
tercets, haikus, tankas,
not to mention villanelles,
terzanelles and rondelets;
conversant with the phonetic
kinships of rhyme, assonance
and consonance; the four
nuances of stress, the three
junctions; forget now
the skeltonic couplet,
the heroic couplet, the split
couplet, the poulter's measure;
speak not of englyn
penfyr, englyn milwr;
but westward hasten
to that rising, lonely ground
between the evening rivers,
the alder-gazing rivers,
Mawddach and Dysynni.

Let it be dark when, alone,
you climb the awful mountain
so that you can count the stars.
Ignore the giant shufflings
behind you – put out that torch! –
the far intermittent cries
of the nocturnal birds,
if birds they are,
their small screams of torture.

Instead, scholar as you are,
remark the old proverb
how the one who ascends
Cadair Idris at night
comes back in dawn's light
lately mad or a great poet.
Meanwhile, I'll wait here
in this dull room of urine-
flask, weighing-machine,
examination-couch, X-ray screen,
for your return (triumphant
or bizarre) patiently.

Arianrhod

Not Arianrhod of Swansea
who could have become a nun,
not cold-flame Arianrhod?
Once, near poppydrowsing corn,
through the cricket weather
consentiently together;
but twice the quarrels after,
dissonances and disorder,
eye-bright denunciations
from theological Arianrhod,
disinclined Arianrhod,

while two rivers were meeting
at Pontneathvaughan.

Night-war came to Swansea
when the kettle was whistling,
Bowdler lay deeper
in Mumbles' graveyard.
Hurdling fire turned to fire
the things it first charred –
both gone Arianrhod's parents
who wailed with the siren,
that ghost-factory siren;
and later stunned Arianrhod
diminished in hospital,
tongue-rotted in hospital,
because their going was hard.

Do names have destinies?
Today in a chronic ward
another Arianrhod, a schizophrene,
picking the frost from her face.
Then back down the landing
heard myself mumbling – Destiny
itself is a man-made name.
Out through the front gate
but still see her standing
on light-iced linoleum,
that used one, Arianrhod,
figure a matchstick,
flame gone without trace.

The Wife of Columbus

After I made love
to the wife of Christopher Columbus
I woke up. Later, over breakfast,
I consulted a map.
Had I not kissed a birthmark
on the soft inside of her right thigh,
a birthmark that resembled
the contours of an island,
familiar but forgotten?
And yet, not necessarily an island.
Error? Columbus thought he'd reached
the spice-rich coast of India.

I have visited, in real daylight,
Columbus, capital of Ohio,
observed Doric buildings
under island-clouds. I have walked
past the Institute of the Blind
questing for something lost, once seen;
also past the Penitentiary
and the Catholic Cathedral
where tall and short women entered,
some hiding their faces
as she did once when the three ships
set sail from the quay at Palos.

Error. I should have journeyed
to a place not on my itinerary –
Columbus, Georgia, perhaps,
and walked all the moody afternoon
beside the Chattahoochee river

searching for a sign;
or Columbus, Indiana, say,
and waited like one asleep
at its junction of railways
for a train of many windows —
with so many sitting skeletons,
so many skulls staring out.

A Footnote Extended

for Thomas Szasz's Karl Kraus and the Soul Doctors

Dr Szasz, professor, sir,
I read your book.
I won't make criticisms (I could)
but more attention, please,
for Egon Friedman,
born in Vienna, 1878,
of Jewish parents.

Who, insulted, endured.
Who studied in Berlin,
later in Heidelberg:
studied German
studied philosophy
studied natural science;
did not write a treatise
on the whale,

that hunted mammal
posing as a fish.

But returned to Vienna,
changed his visiting card.
Friedell now, not Friedman.
'Hello Dr Friedell,
you're a mensch, Dr Friedell.
Here's a bowl of wax apples,
here's a vase of paper flowers,
here's margarine in a lordly dish.'

He ignored such tauntings.
Tall, he turned the other cheek,
he converted to Christianity –
defended the Gospel
against Mosaic subversion;
attacked the Jewish Science
of Psychoanalysis,
called its practitioners –
Freud, Abraham, Stekel –
'underground blood-suckers'.

Ah, applause now
for the proselyte
so soon to be successful,
so edgily celebrated
under the probing, chalky
spotlight of cabaret-actor,
writer, critic, author of
Cultural History of the Modern Age.

When the Nazis marched
into Austria —
strange amphigouri
of circumstance —
Friedell, in his bachelor room,
walked towards the long mirror,
saw Friedman approaching.
Whispered Friedman,
screamed FRIEDMAN,
and killed himself.

White Balloon

Dear love, Auschwitz made me
more of a Jew than ever Moses did.
But the world's not always with us.
Happiness enters here again tonight
like an unexpected guest
with no memory of the future either;

enters with such an italic emphasis,
jubilant, announcing triumphantly
hey presto and here I am and opening
the June door into our night living room
where under the lampshade's ciliate
an armchair's occupied by a white balloon.
As if there'd been a party.

Of course, Happiness, uninhibited,
will pick it up, his stroking thumb
squeaking a little as he leads us to the hall.
And we shall follow him, too,
when he climbs the lit staircase
towards the landing's darkness,
bouncing bouncing the white balloon
from hand to hand.

It's bedtime; soon we must dream
separately — but what does it matter now
as the white balloon is thrown up high?
Quiet, so quiet, the moon above Masada
and closed, abandoned for the night,
the icecream van at Auschwitz.

A Small Farmhouse Near Brno

What could David Molko do,
in that age of local pogroms
when, forlorn, they appeared in his yard,
those bearded cousins, their wives and children,
who had been fed only on saliva,
the tall and pale and the small and pale,
tearful, destitute, distraught?

'My home's your home,' said Molko,
'the air I breathe will be the air
you breathe. As Ben Azzai promised,
you'll be called by your name,
you'll be given what is yours,
you'll be seated in your place.'

And that first night, near or at the table,
they all sang solemnly, even the children,
to the mournful tune of the Hatikvah:
'Austria, Rumania and Russia too,
all combine to persecute the Jew.'
Then all sat to eat of Molko's meat,
then all stood to drink from Molko's cup.

But it came to pass, nights moonlit or moonless,
they did not sing. Instead, discordances,
small quarrels, nags, weepings, sulks,
gnashing of teeth. For fifteen heads slept
in a farmhouse meant for three or four
and even Molko's equable wife
loudly whispered, 'In the belly
of the fish, Jonah, afflicted,
had more room than we have here.'

Molko, being Molko, consulted the rabbi,
the very old, quivering rabbi,
wise as Shammai, as Hillel even.
He said,
          'Behold, you have chickens, Molko,

white chickens and brown chickens,
in the yard you have chickens.
Therefore I say unto you, Molko,
take them into the house also,
the white and the brown chickens,
those that lay white eggs and
those that lay brown eggs.'

Molko, dubiously, took in the chickens.
And it was worse. Only three nights later
he woke from a nightmare shouting,
'More air, more air.' So, at the hour
when great kings set forth to battle,
Molko once more came unto that rabbi
wise as Shammai, as Hillel even,
who said,
      'Behold, you have four goats, Molko.
I have seen them in your yard.
Though not writ in the chronicles
of the kings of Israel I say unto you
take them in, take the four goats in also.'

Molko stared at the palms of his hands.
But the rabbi told how things bitter
can be made sweet, how the lupine
when diligently boiled, soaked seven times
in water, is made so – as mustard is
or the astringent caper-plant.

So Molko took in the goats,
even the very smelly one he called Buz, the son

of the billy goat Guzi, the son of Toah,
the son of Zuph, the son of Asaph.
And it was worse.

'O Lord hear,' cried Molko's agitated wife
and 'O Lord forgive,' and 'O Lord
hearken and do.' So that after three sabbaths
Molko came once more unto the rabbi
who said,
       'Behold, you have no oxen, Molko,
you have no mules, but you own a donkey.
How manifold are Thy works, O Lord.
Yes, take the donkey who trembles like I do
into your sanctuary. As the Lord liveth,
and as I have two changes of garments,
all will be well, trust me, believe me.'

Thus Molko took into his farmhouse
the donkey that stared at the stinking goats,
that stared at the twelve feathered fowl,
the brown ones and the white ones.
And it was worse.

All fifteen in the little house,
the bearded ones and the unbearded ones,
screamed that it was worse, it was much worse –
like after the desolation of Sodom
and, possibly, Gomorrah.

Now Molko came unto the rabbi
crying, 'Woe, woe,' and his right eye runneth

with water and his left eye runneth
with water. So the rabbi pondered
who had studied all the sages of Israel
and said,
      'Behold, I shall deliver thee.
Take out the donkey, yes, take it out
though like me the donkey feels cold
even in June.'

Molko took the donkey out
into the yard, the uncomprehending donkey.
And it was better. But still
the house quarrelled, gnashed its teeth.
So the rabbi stood on one leg
like Hillel, swaying, vibrating,
till wondrously inspired
he said,
      'Behold, take out the four goats
especially Buz, the son
of the billy goat Guzi, the son of Toah,
the son of Zuph, the son of Asaph.'
And lo, Molko obeyed.
And it was better.

But still the house lacked oxygen:
the crying of the children,
the shouting of the women,
the cursing of the bearded ones,
so the rabbi, the very old and wise rabbi
called out,
      'Behold, take out the chickens,

take out the brown ones and the white ones' –
and lo, when the fowl were back in the yard
it was better, oh yes it was better,
and everybody was happy,
so that all now cried out,

'Blessed be the Lord for we are rich,'
and suddenly, it seemed, the little farmhouse
had the height of cedars.
Then they sang near or at the table,
'Austria, Rumania and Russia too,
all combine to persecute the Jew.'

Staring at a Chandelier

True ancestors of mine,
those in hell, those in heaven,
they're not big wheels
like roaring, war-loving Antara.
They've been allocated
only small, menial jobs,
nothing extraordinary.

In hell,
they're working in the boiler-rooms,
fags scuttling for the great stokers
(dry in the air, plain H_2S);

in hell they're tea-boys for the damned
cigar-smoking disc jockeys
who play otitis media pop music.

In heaven
they're mere storekeepers for the harps
(subtle perfumes of jasmine and ambergris);
in heaven they're brushing down
angel wings or polishing the haloes
– the standard, economy type,
not the real, business-class, gold ones.

How do I know all this,
I, inappropriately dressed
in my one and only suit
(now visibly fatigued, tight-fitting)
kept for formal occasions,
for functions and funerals
of the last twenty-five years?

I had the sense of it in the queue
when the six-foot-four flunkey
shouted, 'Her Highness, the Duchess of This,'
and 'Air Vice-Marshal What,'
and 'General Hyphenated-Why,'
and 'Lord and Lady That,'
then asked me, three times, to repeat my name.

Soon after, I saw it in the predictable
dazzle of a chandelier
high above those ageing folk

gathering in gowns and uniforms
on the red carpet under it
and who, when next I looked,
like the tall flunkey, had vanished.

Brueghel in Naples

About suffering they were never wrong,
The Old Masters . . . W. H. Auden

Ovid would never have guessed how far
and Father's notion about wax melting, bah!
It's ice up there. Freezing.
Soaring and swooping over solitary altitudes
I was breezing along (a record I should think)
when my wings began to moult not melt.
These days, workmanship, I ask you.
Appalling.
There's a mountain down there on fire
and I'm falling, falling away from it.
Phew, the sun's on the horizon
or am I upside down?

Great Bacchus, the sea is rearing
up. Will I drown? My white legs
the last to disappear? (I have no trousers on.)
A little to the left the ploughman,
a little to the right a galleon,

a sailor climbing the rigging,
a fisherman casting his line,
and now I hear a shepherd's dog barking.
I'm that near.

Lest I leave no trace
but a few scattered feathers on the water
show me your face, sailor,
look up, fisherman,
look this way, shepherd,
turn around, ploughman.
Raise the alarm! Launch a boat!

My luck. I'm seen
only by a jackass of an artist
interested in composition, in the green
tinge of the sea, in the aesthetics
of disaster – not in me.

I drown, bubble by bubble,
(Help! Save me!)
while he stands ruthlessly
before the canvas, busy busy,
intent on becoming an Old Master.

The Green Field

As soft-eyed lovers for the very first time,
turning out the light for the first time,
blot out all detail, all colours,
and whisper the old code-words, 'Love you',

so those admiring that patch of grass,
there, on the hillside, from this distance
could be in the dark, unconcerned with detail.
'That green field,' they generalize,

though drawing nearer (as to a poem)
they will discover the lies of distance:
rage of different greens. And at the field itself
an unforeseen tapestry of variousness:

sprawl of common weeds and wild flowers,
subtleties of small petals seldom green.

Condensation on a Windowpane

I

I want to write something simple,
something simple, a few adjectives,
ambiguities disallowed.

Something old fashioned:
a story of Time perhaps
or, more daringly, of love.

I want to write something simple
that everyone can understand,
something simple as pure water.

But pure water
is H_2O
and that's complicated
like steam, like ice, like clouds.

2

My finger squeaks on glass.
I write JOAN
I write DANNIE.
Imagine! I'm a love-struck
youth again.

I want to say something
without ambiguity.
Imagine! Me, old-age pensioner
wants to say something
to do with love and Time,
love that's simple as water.

But long ago we learnt
water is complicated,
is H_2O, is ice, is steam, is cloud.

Our names on the window
begin to fade.
Slowly, slowly.
They weep as they vanish.

The Excavation

Absurd those tall stories of tall heroes.
Mine, too. Sixty ells, they said, between
my shoulders! Happy legends of my strength!
Hippy myths of my hair! How I lifted up
a mountain here, a mountain there. Dig, dig:
so little recorded, so many exaggerations.

Three hundred foxes, they said, remember?
Nine, only nine. With a jawbone of an ass,
they said, I topped a thousand men. Dig, dig
for their gritty skulls. I unthatched a mere ten.
Let others boast that I was 'magic',
the rainbow spirit of the Lord about me.

But absent, He, when the whips cracked and I
was led, eyeless, into Dagon's Temple,
heard the hooting crazies on the roof, So many,
the junk Temple collapsed thunderously.
Joke! They thought *I'd* brought the House down –
me, clapped-out circus act, defunct Strong Man.

I was screaming, believe me, I was lost.
Betrayed, betrayed, and so little recorded:
the brevities of a Hebrew scribe only;
a fable for a Milton to embroider;
a picture for a Rubens to paint;
music for the soul of a Saint-Saëns.

Dig, dig, though you will not find Dagon's
stone fish-tail nor the scissors of the sung star
of the Philistines. Who knows the path of that whore
after the Temple, unglued, crashed and crushed?
Did she return to Sorek or raise once more
her aprons in the brothels of Philistia?

Dig, dig. I hear your questing spades muffled,
south of Gaza. Useless. The shifting sands
have buried deeper the graves of all.
Only the wilderness remains, silence
and a jawbone. And marvellous ghosts
people a yellow page of Judges.

History

(*To Peter Vansittart*)

The last war-horse slaughtered and eaten
long ago. Not a rat, not a crow-crumb

left; the polluted water scarce;
the vile flies settling on the famous
enlarged eyes of skeleton children.

Tonight the moon's open-mouthed. I must
surrender in the morning. But those
cipher tribes out there, those Golden Hordes,
those shit! They'll loot and maim and rape.
What textbook atrocities in the morning?

Now, solitary, my hip-joint aching,
half-lame, I climb the high battlements
carrying a musical instrument.
Why not? What's better? The bedlam of sleep
or the clarities of insomnia?

Look! Below, most fearful perspective:
cloud-fleeing shadows of unending
flatlands; enemy tent after tent
pegged to the unstable moonlight.
You'd think the moon, exposed, would howl.

Besieged city, in some future
history book (aseptic page or footnote)
they'll fable your finale: how
your huck-shouldered, arthritic General,
silhouette on the dark battlements,

played on his pipe a Mongolian song,
an enemy song, played so purely

the Past disrobed, memory made audible,
(sharp as a blade, lonely, most consequent,
that soul-naked melody of the steppes);

how, below, the Mongol soldiers awoke,
listened, leaned on their elbows tamed,
became so utterly homesick, wretched,
so inflamed, that by the cold sweats
of dawnlight, they decamped, departed.

Ha! Such a pleasing, shameless story,
to be told over and over by these
and by those: by propagandists of music;
by descendants of the Mongols.
But, alas, only a scribe's invention.

The truth? I play pianissimo
and not very well. The sleepers
in their tents sleep on, the sentries
hardly stir. I loiter on the battlements.
Stars! Stars! I put away my pipe and weep.

Meurig Dafydd to His Mistress

No word I huffed when Stradling urged the squire
to throw my eulogy on the fire.

The fiddlers laughed. I, snow-silent, proud,
did not melt. But I'm spitless now,
my pearl, my buttercup, my bread-fruit.
I rattle their silver in my pocket.
I have other stanzas for harp and lute,
other gullible lords to flatter.
What do I care for that big-bellied Englishman,
that bugle, that small-beer, that puff-ball,
that dung-odoured sonneteer, John Stradling?

Does he sing perfect metre like Taliesin?
Not that gout-toed, goat-faced manikin.
What does he know of Welsh necks crayoned
by the axe, blood on our feet, our history?
Has he stood pensive at the tomb
of Morien, or Morial, or March?
Wept at any nervous harp, at the gloom
of a dirge for Llywelyn the Last,
or the lament by Lewis Glyn Cothi?
That fungoid, that bunt, that broken-wind,
that bog-bean, can't tell a song from a grunt.

Clean heart, my theology, my sweet-briar,
he'd put our heritage on the fire.
Each night he swigs mead in a safe bed –
never sleeps roofed only by the stars.
At noon, never signs the euphonious nine
sermons of the blackbird. O my lotus,
his lexicon is small compared to mine.
His verses are like standing urine – tepid.

My Welsh stanzas have more heat in them
than the tumbling flames in the fire-place
of the Minstrel Hall of Bewpyr.

Ya

The machine began to hum.
Some blood, they pleaded,
just a little, uncoagulated,
fresh blood, please.
It was springtime, springtime,
the season to open doors.
A pinprick? On the thumb?
They shook their heads.
Hesitant, scrupulous,
sullenly, we detached a finger
– under an anaesthetic,
humanely, you understand.
But, afterwards, candid,
they demanded, More blood!
And, ya, after debate
we did amputate a hand:
soft tissues retracted,
joint opened cleanly,
lateral ligaments cut through.
From the wrist.
Better, they said hoarsely,

leaving us discomfited.
What else could we do?
Outside it was springtime, springtime,
the birds' hullabaloo;
the young cried as usual,
not knowing why,
the old because they knew.
So, ya, a whole arm,
almost a perfect job
and without an anaesthetic too.
No wonder they applauded,
their obscene shouts, their keen whistles,
like hosannas from hell.
Allow us this though;
outside it was shifting sunlight,
it was wild bluebells
and, ya, one of us at the window
quoted an English poet-priest:
I do not think I've seen
anything more beautiful
than a bluebell.
I know the beauty
of our Lord by it.
So not till all the women
were released, banished,
did we consent to saw off
a raw foot. Right and left neatly,
our technique swift, improving.
And who could not respond
excitedly – that adrenal flow –
to their rhythmic chanting?

Ya, with both legs wide
then unhinged completely,
oh the powerful voltage
of their male applause
and oh the soulful thrilling
of our National Anthem.
So moving, so very moving,
man it was something.
Fellow scientists,
you can guess
what happened next,
ya, you know
the end of the story.

Beautiful Dead Poets

She spoke of Garcia Lorca murdered;
Hernandez dying in a Franco prison;
Mayakovsky's suicide; how Mandelstam
jumped through the window of a hospital;
Celan and Levi in the Nazi Death Camps.
'Beautiful dead poets, all of them,' said she,
in the delight of enthusiasm.

Behind her, a dark mahogany table
that once had the girth of a lofty tree;

a vase of deep red, drooping lovely things –
aged tulips – untimely ripped from the earth;
and, by the window, a canary caged
because it sang so beautifully.

Ghosting for Mayakovsky

(His suicide note)

I

It's long past one and you must be asleep.
The quiet night's astonished by all the stars.
Why wake you now with a telegram like thunder?

So many thoughts of mystery the night can bring.
Dear love, our love boat's on the rocks. Its sails
wrenched from the mast. No use in adding up the cost,

we're quits; no need to weigh our hearts and hurts
upon the scales. 'No Life without you,' once I said,
and now the strokes of Two thud down like heads from blocks.

Our story's over, iconoclast. I'm lost. I'm through.
No need to wake you with a telegram like thunder.
Art's imperative will make these lines come true.

Once I drew the Queen of Hearts,
now I'm dealt another card. A club. A two.
Once forbidden love lit up like paper burning
then it charred.

Once with verse of lightning and half in song
I told a daisy and the world
you loved me, you love me not,
and how worthless life unfurled would be
without you – like a single shoe.
I'll not limp along.

I'm shot. I'm through.
Queen of Hearts, O Queen of Hearts,
the imperatives of Art insist,
the lies of Art come true.

Cricket Ball

1935, I watched Glamorgan play
especially Slogger Smart, free
from the disgrace of fame, unrenowned,
but the biggest hit with me.

A three-spring flash of willow
and suddenly, the sound of summer
as the thumped ball, alive, would leave
the applauding ground.

Once, hell for leather, it curled
over the workman's crane
in Westgate Street
to crash, they said, through a discreet
Angel Hotel windowpane.

But I, a pre-war boy,
(or someone with my name)
wanted it, that Eden day,
to scoot around the turning world,
to mock physics and gravity,
to rainbow-arch the posh hotel
higher, deranged, on and on, allegro,
(the Taff a gleam of mercury below)
going, going, gone
towards the Caerphilly mountain range.

Vanishings! The years, too, gone like change.
But the travelling Taff seems the same.
It's late. I peer at the failing sky
over Westgate Street
and wait. I smell cut grass.
I shine an apple on my thigh.

Two Photographs

Here's a photograph of grandmother, Annabella.
How slim she appears, how vulnerable. Pretty.
And here's a photograph of grandmother, Doris.
How portly she looks, formidable. Handsome.
Annabella wears a demure black frock with an amber brooch.
Doris, a lacy black gown with a string of pearls.
One photo's marked *Ystalyfera* 1880,
the other *Bridgend* 1890.
Both were told to say, 'Cheese'; one, defiant, said 'Chalk!'

Annabella spoke Welsh with a Patagonian accent.
Doris spoke English with a Welsh Valleys lilt.
Annabella fasted – pious, passive, enjoyed small-talk.
Doris feasted – pacy, pushy, would never pray. Ate pork!
When Annabella told Doris she was damned
indecorous Doris devilishly laughed.
I liked Doris, I liked Annabella,
though Doris was bossy and Annabella daft.
I do not think they liked each other.

Last night I dreamed they stood back to back,
not for the commencement of a duel
but to see who was taller! Now, in these revived
waking hours, my Eau de Cologne grandmothers
with buns of grey hair, of withered rose,
seem illusory, fugitive, like my dream –
or like the dust that secretively flows
in a sudden sunbeam (sieved through leaky curtains)
and disappears when and where that sunbeam goes.

Of two old ladies once uxoriously loved,
what's survived? An amber brooch, a string of pearls,
two photographs. Happening on them, my children's
grandchildren will ask 'Who?' – hardly aware
that if this be not true, I never lived.

In the Villa Borghese

The chase. Through the wood, the terror of it.
The choice. Violent love or vegetable asylum.
Still true, sometimes, for uncertain men.
Still true, sometimes, for certain women.
She, with the soul of a nun, chose.

In the Villa Borghese they have become marble.
Millions of days, millions of nights
they pose. He, too, ironically petrified.

With a stethoscope I want to hear
their two hearts beat within the marble.
I want to put a mirror to their mouths.

According to Ovid, she chose. Who cried?
She left him priapic and aching.
Did it rain then? Did he lift his god's leg?

Now I hear, outside, the seminal patter of it
on wide laurel leaves. No matter,
a tree might welcome such fresh drenching.

A feminist victory? Hardly.
True, one more heavy breather denied –
unless, of course, Ovid, pleasing some prim,
some god-loving, soma-loathing priest,
sweetened an older, raunchier story. Lied.

Destinies

(To Francis Celoria)

Sometimes the gods appear to be insane.
So addicted to metamorphosis!
Pity the unloved vulture flying above a roof,
pity the lone eagle settling on a mountain.

Long ago, 'Hail Periphas!' cried the populace
and built a great temple in his honour;
began to call him, 'Overlooker of All'
and at the agora, 'Your Imperial Grace',

offending big-jawed Zeus. His boss-face gorged
with anger – he, flash lord of the thunderbolts,
scandalous incinerator of men –
bridled his ten white horses and charged

over boiling plains towards the Aegean shore
where that afternoon, in sand-dune amour,
Periphas, anastomosing with Phene, sighed,
'Dear one,' while she replied, 'Love evermore!'

Four times unignorable Zeus tapped
the busy bare back of rapt Periphas.
Alas, when Periphas turned he was turned
into a bird, into an eagle that flapped

its wings till Phene, flushed, opened her eyes.
First, surprise. Then appalling cries were heard;
but still she, faithful wife, begged to become
bird also. 'Please Judicious One, All-wise.'

Praised, the god, red-toothed, smiled. Would he concur?
Her nakedness fled and she was covered
with feathers till, heart and head, Phene was
all bird, all sorry-looking vulture.

The sweetness of feminine self-denial!
Are male saints, unmasked, deceiving women?
Other men become wolves to savage other men
so who'd arraign Zeus? Put the gods on trial?

They pester with vipers the sleep of mankind
and, like men, won't forgive those they've injured.
What horrors have they in mind, what transformations
in the zoo of Time to come? To prove unkind?

Sometimes the gods cannot remain aloof
when the populace love a man too much.
Pity the lone eagle flying about a mountain.
Pity the unloved vulture settling on a roof.

Touch Wood

Come, let us praise wood
no longer agrestial.
Not the trillions of coffins
but wood within a living house,
the quietude of an empty bookcase,
the loneliness of scattered chairs –
the metamorphosis
of trees, shrubs, bushes, twigs.
Doors particularly, upstairs, downstairs,
whatever their disposition,
welcoming, half open,
or secretively shut.

It does not matter.
Delightful the craftsmanship
of their lintels,
so comely, so pleasant,
like the repeated oblongs
of windowframes, upstairs, downstairs,
like the serenity of windowsills

that carry vases, flower-pots.
And who could not respond
to the utilitarian elegance
of a wide staircase
rising from a parquet floor?

What a history wood has,
what old echoing stories
in the random museum of the mind:
the gopher ark of Noah
floating high above the mountains;
the huge, staring Trojan horse;
Diogenes's fat barrel;
Horatius's one-way bridge
that fell into the Tiber;
King Arthur's Round Table —
all these relics lost forever
like Jesus's insensate Cross.

Sometimes I think we should construct
in the garden of a living house
an idol of various woods:
head of Lombardy Poplar,
trunk of reliable Oak,
arms of Elm and Pine,
hands of Lime and Plane,
legs of Birch and Beech,
feet of grainy Sycamore
and genitals (of course, discreet)
of musty Fig tree, untidy Fir
and the droopy Weeping Willow.

November nights when we're asleep,
when unbuttoned winds shake the house,
what the spirit of the house
if not the spirit of the forest?
What replies if not primal wood,
dryad-ghost and Daphne-creak,
wild cries of wood awakening?
We, stern-faced as mourners, slumber on,
carry in dream the golden bough
from some black forgotten tree
of the windless underworld
back to the leaf-strewn morning.

Thankyou Note

for the unbidden swish of morning curtains
you opened wide – letting sleep-baiting shafts
of sunlight enter to lie down by my side;
for adagio afternoons when you did the punting
(my toiling eyes researched the shifting miles of sky);
for back-garden evenings when you chopped the wood
and I, incomparably, did the grunting;
(a man too good for this world of snarling
is no good for his wife – truth's the safest lie);

for applauding my poetry, O most perceptive spouse;
for the improbable and lunatic, my darling;

for amorous amnesties after rancorous rows
like the sweet-nothing whisperings of a leafy park
after the blatant noise of a city street
(exit booming cannons, enter peaceful ploughs);
for kindnesses the blind side of my night-moods;
for lamps you brought in to devour the dark.

On the Evening Road

A disgrace a man of my age
to have come this far and not to know;
the fields inert with ignorant mist,
the road between, lost, unsignposted.

I may as well sing a little
since no-one's around to hear me,
'The Song of Omega' my father sang
though the words I've mostly forgotten.

I may as well dance a bit, too,
since no-one's around to scold me:
'Disgrace, a man of his age singing
drunkenly – not knowing where he is.'

Now the Caladrius bird lands
as it must, on the road ahead of me

and drops its dung. Turn towards me, bird,
O turn, turn, with your yellow beak.

St Valentine's Night

Eros, immutable archer, one eye closed,
you let your arrows fly. It was St Valentine's
night, I remember. For me the first time. The Cardiff
moon was flirting with a cloud, its light discreet,
and I with a box of Black Magic chocolates
and she with such a healthy appetite.

Homage to Eros! Slow and sensual the sweet
unwrapping, the soft-centred she coming into sight.
St Valentine, himself, would have been up
to make her, with her fallen party dress
rustling on the rug like classy chocolate paper.

Be with me still, jubilant Eros, life-saver,
necessary ally. The other gods only wound
the world and scowling Thanatos keeps trying
to recite the 11th commandment: Thou shalt die.
It was St Valentine's night, I remember.
You plucked your great bow then, Eros. Pluck it now.

Marzipan. Cherry Liqueur. Turkish Delight.

O Taste and See

Because of a kiss on the forehead
in the long Night's infirmary,
through the red wine let light shine deep.

Because of the thirtysix just men
that so stealthily roam this earth
raise high the glass and do not weep.

Who says the world is not a wedding?
Couples, in their oases, lullabye.
Let glass be full before they sleep.

Toast all that which seems to vanish
like a rainbow stared at, those bright
truant things that will not keep;

and ignorance of the last night
of our lives, its famished breathing.
Then, in the red wine, taste the light.

At the Albert Hall

Anarchic dissonances first, so that
somewhere else a lonely scarecrow shivers
in a winter field. A mortician's crow
perches on its head. It begins to snow.
They bring the scarecrow indoors. They feed it

with phosphorus so it should glow at night.
A great orchestra's tuning-up is ghost talk.

The wand! Then the sudden tamed silence of
a cemetery. Who dares to blackly cough?
Threatened, the conductor raises both arms,
an invisible gun pressed to his back.
Listen. And they speak of the sweet psalmist
of Israel, of 200 loaves of bread
and of 100 bundles of raisins.

Photograph and White Tulips

A little nearer please. And a little nearer
we move to the window, to the polished table.
Objects become professional: mannequins
preening themselves before an audience. Only
the tulips, self-absorbed, ignore the camera.

All photographs flatter us if we wait
long enough. So we awkwardly Smile please
while long-necked tulips, sinuous out of the vase,
droop over the polished table. They're entranced
by their own puffed and smudgy reflections.

Hold it! Click. Once more! And we smile again
at one who'll be irrevocably absent.

Quick. Be quick! the tulips, like swans, will dip
their heads deep into the polished table
frightening us. Thank you. And we turn thinking,

What a fuss! Yet decades later, dice thrown,
we'll hold it, thank you, this fable of gone
youth (was that us?) and we shall smile please
and come a little nearer to the impetuous
once-upon-a-time that can never be twice.

(Never never be twice!) Yet we'll always recall
how white tulips, quick quick, changed into swans
enthralled, drinking from a polished table.
As for those white petals, they'll never fall
in that little black coffin now carrying us.

The Boasts of Hywel ab Owain Gwynedd

Sunday, skilled in zealous verse I praise the Lord.
Monday, I sing in bed to my busty Nest,
'Such whiteness you are, pear blossom must be jealous.'
Tuesday, scholar Gwladus. Not to love her is a sin.
My couplets she pigeon-coos when I thrust to woo her
till her pale cheeks flush like rosy apple skin.
Wednesday, Generys. Dry old hymns I steal to please her.
Then with passion fruit in season I kneel to ease her.

199

Thursday, Hunydd, no hesitating lady, she.
One small cherry-englyn and she's my devotee.
Friday, worried Hawis, my epic regular.
She wants no baby, she's gooseberry vehement
till sugared by my poetry of endearment.
Saturday, I score and score. One tidy eulogy
and I'm away – I can't brake – through an orchard
I adore. O sweet riot of efflorescence,
let her name be secret for her husband's sake,
my peach of a woman, my vegetarian diet.

O tongue, lick up juices of the fruit. O teeth
– I've all of mine – be sure my busy tongue keeps quiet.

Lament of Heledd

(based on a fragment of a 9th century Welsh saga poem)

I

I had four brothers. A pike upholds the head
of noble Cynddylan. The corn is red.

I had four brothers. Cynon and Gwiawn
butchered in the straw, their swords not drawn.

Four brothers I had. Vague, hesitant Gwyn
last to fall. Through his neck a javelin.

When will this brute night end? Where shall I go?
Morning's mortuary will be kitchen for the crow.

II

Cynddylan's Hall is dark tonight.
The stone stairs lead nowhere. No candle glows
behind the lower then the higher windows.

Cynddylan's Hall is dark tonight
and dark the smoke rising from its ruin.
Slain, slain, are Cynddylan and all our kin.

Cynddylan's Hall is dark tonight,
its great roof burnt down, I can see the stars.
Curse those Englishmen, their bloody wars.

Cynddylan's Hall is dark tonight.
No orison is wailed to harp or lute.
O ghost brothers, your sister's destitute.

Cynddylan's Hall is dark tonight,
its silence outrageous. I shall go mad.
I smell skeletons. O blood of my blood.

Cynddylan's Hall is dark tonight.
Should I live on? I am no heroine.
O Cynddylan, Cynon, Gwiawn, and Gwyn.

Welsh Valley Cinema, 1930s

In The Palace of the slums,
from the Saturday night pit,
from an unseen shaft of darkness
I remember it: how, first, a sound
took wing grandly; then the thrill
of a fairground sight – it rose,
lordly stout thing, boasting
a carnival of gaudy-bright,
changing colours while wheezing out
swelling rhonchi of musical asthma.

I hear it still, played with panache
by renowned gent, Cathedral Jones,
'When the Broadway Baby Says Goodnight
it's Early in the Morning' – then he and it
sank to disappear, a dream underground.

Later, those downstairs, gobbing silicosis
(shoeless feet on the mecca carpet),
observed a miracle – the girl next door,
a poor ragged Goldilocks,
dab away her glycerine tears
to kiss cuff-linked Cary Grant
under an elegance of chandeliers.
(No flies on Cary. No holes in *his* socks.)

And still the Woodbine smoke swirled on
in the opium beam of the operator's box
till THE END – of course, upbeat.
Then from The Palace, the damned Fall,
the glum, too silent trooping out

into the trauma of paradox:
the familiar malice of the dreary,
unemployed, gas-lamped street
and the striking of the small Town's clocks.

Sixth-Form Poet

When my acne almost cleared
I fell in love with humankind.
I wanted to requisition Poetry,
a revolution in my mind.

To the barricades not the court,
my gorgeous rage would console.
Though love be blind it sees
with the optic nerve of the soul.

Poetry is written in the brain
but the brain is bathed in blood.
I sang no praises for the King,
I, laureate to Robin Hood.

A Heritage

A heritage of a sort.
A heritage of comradeship and suffocation.

The bawling pit-hooter and the god's
explosive foray, vengeance, before retreating
to his throne of sulphur.
Now this black-robed god of fossils
and funerals,
petrifier of underground forests
and flowers,
emerges with his grim retinue
past a pony's skeleton, past human skulls,
into his half-propped up, empty, carbon colony.

Above, on the brutalized,
unstitched side of a Welsh mountain,
it has to be someone from somewhere else
who will sing solo

not of the marasmus of the Valleys,
the pit-wheels that do not turn,
the pump-house abandoned;

nor of how, after a half-mile fall
regiments of miners' lamps
no longer, midge-like,
rise and slip and bob.

Only someone uncommitted,
someone from somewhere else,
panorama-high on a coal-tip

may jubilantly laud
the re-entry of the exiled god
into his shadowless kingdom.

He, drunk with methane,
raising a man's femur like a sceptre;
she, his ravished queen,
admiring the blood-stained black roses
that could not thrive on the plains of Enna.

Souls

'After the last breath, eyelids must be closed
quickly. For eyes are windows of the soul
– that shy thing which is immortal. And none
should see its exit vulnerably exposed,'

proclaimed the bearded man on Yom Kippur.
Grown-ups believed in the soul. Otherwise
why did grandfather murmur the morning prayer,
'Lord, the soul Thou hast given me is pure'?

Near the kitchen door where they notched my height
a mirror hung. There I saw the big eyes
of a boy. I could not picture the soul
immaterial and immortal. A cone of light?

Those two black zeros the soul's windows? Daft!
Later, at medical school, I learnt of
the pineal gland, its size a cherry-stone,
vestige of the third eye, and laughed.

But seven colours hide in light's disguise
and the blue sky's black. No wonder Egyptians
once believed, in their metamorphosis,
souls soared, became visible: butterflies.

Now old, I'm credulous. Superstition clings.
After the melting eyes and devastation
of Hiroshima, they say butterflies, crazed,
flew about, fluttering soundless things.

My Neighbour, Itzig

My neighbour, Itzig,
has gone queer with religion.
Yesterday he asked me
who named the angels!

Today his dog is barking and barking.

But like music that's ceased
in an adjoining room

Itzig is not here,
He is nowhere else, either.

Itzig, listen, your dog needs a walk.

But Itzig is droning on and on
– open the window, someone –
a prayer archaic and musty
and full of O.

His sad feet are on this earth,
his happy head is elsewhere
among the configuration
of the 7 palaces of light.

Come back, Itzig, your dog needs feeding.

But Itzig quests for the 8th colour.
His soul is cartwheeling, he's far
from the barely manageable
drama of the Present Tense.

Come back, Itzig, your dog needs water.

But Itzig follows, with eyes closed,
the footsteps of the sages
Amora and Rehumai
who never existed.

A Letter from Ogmore-by-Sea

Goodbye, 20th Century.
What should I mourn?
Hiroshima? Auschwitz?
Our friend, Carmi, said,
'Thank forgetfulness
else we could not live;
thank memory
else we'd have no life.'

Goodbye, 20th Century.
What shall I celebrate?
Darling, I'm out of date:
even my nostalgia
is becoming history.
Those garish, come-on posters
outside a cinema,
announce the Famous
I've never heard of.
So many other friends, too,
now like Carmi, have joined
a genealogy of ghosts.

But here, this mellow evening,
on these high cliffs I look down
to read the unrolling
holy scrolls of the sea. They are
blank. The enigma is alive
and, for the Present, I boast,
thumbs in lapels, I survive.

Delightful Eros
still hauls Reason along
zig-zag on a taut leash.
I'm still unsettled by
the silence in framed pictures,
foreground and background;
or the mastery of music
over mind. And I hail
the world within a word.
I do not need to be
a fabulist like Iolo
who, from this same coast,
would see seven sails
where there was but one.

Goodbye, 20th Century,
your trumpets and your drums,
your war-wounds still unhealed.
Goodbye, I-must-leave-you-Dolly,
goodbye Lily Marlene.
Has the Past always a future?
Will there always be
a jackboot on the stair,
a refugee to roam?
A man with no roots is lost
like the darkness in the forest
and it costs 100 years
for a hiding place
to become a home.

Now secular strangers come
sealed in Fords and Nissans,
a congregation of cars,
to this opening estuary
so various, so beautiful, so old.
The tide *is* out.
And from the sleeping
reeled-in sea – not from
the human mind's vexed fathoms –
the eternal, murderous,
fanged Tusker Rock is revealed.

Useful Knowledge

Shy Colin, the most silent of men
despite his ammunition of facts.
He'd bomb them out at dinner parties
before signing off from conversation.

'The mastrich tree, as you probably know,
is brown, resinous, and most fragrant.'
'Volapuk? Nobody speaks it now.
Lost its one thousand, five hundred words.'

At Anne's, he said, 'Tortoises often die
from diphtheria.' At our place, he told us

'Lake Titicaca's half the size of Wales –
half's in Bolivia, half in Peru.'

Last April, when his two-year-old son
lay big-eyed in the Royal Infirmary,
Colin heard the consultant whisper
to his Registrar, 'Nieman-Pick Disease.'

Colin closed his eyes, cried out shrilly,
'A genetically determined disorder
where splenectomy is palliative.
Death occurs quite early during childhood.'

Child Drawing in a Hospital Bed

Any child can open wide
the occult doors of a colour
naively to call, 'Who's there?'
For this sick girl drawing
outstep invisible ones
imprisoned everywhere.
Wasp on a windowpane.

Darkest tulip her head bends,
face white as leukaemia,
till the prince in his tower,

on parole from a story,
descends by royal crayon
and, thrilled, stays half an hour.
Wasp on a windowpane.

Birds of Rhiannon, pencilled,
alight to wake the dead –
they do not sing, she rubs them out,
they smudge into vanishings,
they swoop to Nowhere
as if disturbed by a shout.
Wasp on a windowpane.

Omens. Wild astrologies whirl:
sun and moon begin to soar.
Unlikely that maroon sky
green Christmas trees fly through
– doctors know what logic's for.
Tell me, what is magic for?
Wasp on a windowpane.

Now penal-black she profiles
four eerie malformed horses,
nostrils tethered to the ground.
Unperturbed, the child attends
for one to uplift its neck
and turn its death's head round.
Wasp on a windowpane.

Presences

I'm halted by the unintentional
honeyed malice of mementos:
this awkward night-school painting
by my genial father-in-law;
this vast desk my mother fussed
to give me. 'Fit for an emperor!'

And here's another hook to chin:
a door opens in the next room
and I hear a snatch of Gershwin –
that tune our car-bound family used
to sing. On music's heartless beat
my keen dead come marching in.

O button-holing familiars,
your blurs I sense, your ashes I taste.
So much I owe, so much forgotten
that I owe. But now dear ghosts go
that I may live. Be brief guests.
Leave with a burglar's haste.

The future's future is another place
where other absences will sting; where
some unfocused progeny perhaps
will summon me, stumbling on
some inherited thing or, less likely,
reading this poem, maybe!

Inscription on the Flyleaf of a Bible

(For Larne)

Doubting, read what this fabled history teaches,
how the firework, Imagination, reaches high
to dignify and sanctify.

You need not, granddaughter, be religious
to learn what Judges, Kings, Prophets, yield,
thought-lanterns for Life's darker field,
moral lies of piety and poetry.

You need not, granddaughter, hosanna heroes:
this wily shepherd, that bloodthirsty tough;
yet applaud the bulrush child
who, when offered gold, chose the coal.
Satisfied, the tyrant Pharaoh smiled,
did not see the pattern in the whole.

Forgive the triumphalism and the pride,
forgo the curses and the ritual stuff.
You, older, I hope, will always side
with the enslaved and hunted,
deride the loud and lethal crowd
who vilify and simplify.

What is poetry but the first words
Adam, amazed, spoke to Eve?
On the first page of Genesis
hear the next to Nothing.
Later sound-effects, God off-stage, or theurgic stunts,
(water from a rock, a bush ablaze) might deceive
but bring ladders only to nerveless heaven.

Better to walk with Jephthah's luckless daughter
among real hills. And grieve.

Enjoy David's winging gifts to praise;
Solomon's rapturous serenade; also Job's
night-starred elegance of distress –
though such eloquence can bless,
indiscriminately, the last flags of the just
and the unjust on the barricade.

Read, granddaughter, these scandalous stories,
screaming Joseph in the pit of scorpions,
champion Goliath of course outclassed;
so many cubits of sorrow and delight,
so many visions of our ruffian Past.
They do not stale or fade
and may fortify and mollify.

Events Leading to the Conception of Solomon, the Wise Child

*And David comforted Bathsheba his wife, and went into her, and lay
with her; and she bore a son, and he called his name Solomon: and the
Lord loved him*

I

Are the omina favourable?
Scribes know the King's spittle,

even the most honoured
like Seraiah the Canaanite,
and there are those, addicted,
who inhale
        the smoke of burning papyrus.

So is the date-wine sour, the lemon sweet?
Who can hear the sun's furnace?

The shadow of some great bird
        drifts indolently
across the ochres and umbers
of the afternoon hills
        that surround Jerusalem.
Their rising contours, their heat-refracting
        undulations.

The lizard is on the ledges,
the snake is in the crevices.

It is where Time lives.

Below, within the thermals of the Royal
        City,
past the cursing camel driver,
past the sweating woman carrying water
        in a goatskin,
past the leper peeping through
        the lateral slats
of his fly-mongering latrine

to the walls of the Palace itself,
the chanting King is at prayer.

Aha, aha,
attend to my cry, O Lord
who makest beauty
to be consumed away like a moth;
purge me with hyssop and I
shall be clean.
Wash me and I shall be whiter
than the blossom.
Blot out my iniquities.

Not yet this prayer, not yet
that psalm.
It is where a story begins.
Even the bedouin beside their black tents
have heard the desert wind's rumour.
They ask:
Can papyrus grow
where there is no marsh?
They cry:
Sopher yodea
to the Scribe with two tongues,
urge him to tend his kingdom
of impertinence.

II

When the naked lady stooped to bathe
in the gushings of a spring,

the voyeur on the tower roof
   just happened to be the King.

She was summoned to the Palace
   where the King displayed his charms;
he stroked the harp's glissandos,
   sang her a couple of psalms.

Majestic sweet-talk in the Palace
   – he name-dropped Goliath and Saul –
till only one candle-flame flickered
   and two shadows moved close on the wall.

Of course she hankered for the Palace.
   Royal charisma switched her on.
Her husband snored at the Eastern Front,
   so first a kiss, then scruples gone.

Some say, 'Sweet victim in the Palace,'
   some say, 'Poor lady in his bed.'
But Bathsheba's teeth like milk were white,
   and her mouth like wine was red.

David, at breakfast, bit an apple.
   She, playful, giggling, seized his crown,
then the apple-flesh as usual
   after the bite turned brown.

III

In the kitchen, the gregarious, hovering flies
where the servants breakfast.
A peacock struts
    in its irradiance,
and is ignored.

On the stone floor and on the shelves
the lovely shapes of utensils,
great clay pots, many jugs of wine
    many horns of oil,
the food-vessels and the feast-boards.

On the long table, butter of kine, thin loaves,
bowls of olives and griddle-cakes,
wattled baskets of summer fruit,
flasks of asses' milk and jars of honey.

What a tumult of tongues,
    the maids and the men,
the hewers of wood,
the drawers of water,
    the narrow-skulled
    and the wide-faced.
What a momentary freedom prospers,
    a detour from routine,
a substitute for mild insurrection.

They ask:
  In his arras-hung chamber

did the King smell of the sheepcote?
On the ivory bench, did he seat her
    on cushions?
Did she lie on the braided crimson couch,
beneath her head pillows of goat hair?

Who saw him undo her raiments?
Who overheard Uriah's wife,
Bathsheba of the small voice,
    cry out?
Was it a woman made love to
or the nocturnal moan
    of the turtle dove?
Will the priest, Nathan, awaken
who, even in his sleep, mutters
    Abomination?

Now she who is beautiful to look upon
leaves furtively by a back door.
She will become a public secret.
She wears fresh garments of blue and purple,
the topaz of Ethiopia beneath her apparel.
But a wind gossips in the palm trees,
the anaphora of the wind
    in the fir-trees of Senir,
    in the cedars of Lebanon,
    in the oaks of Bashan.
It flaps the tents where Uriah, the Hittite,
is encamped with Joab's army
on the Eastern open fields.

Does purity of lust last one night only?
In the breakfasting kitchen, the peacock screams.

IV

The wind blows and the page turns over.
   Soon the King was reading a note.
Oh such excruciating Hebrew:
   'I've one in the bin,' she wrote.

Since scandal's bad for royal business
   the King must not father the child;
so he called Uriah from the front,
   shook his hand like a voter. Smiled.

Uriah had scorned the wind's whisper,
   raised his eyebrows in disbelief.
Still, here was the King praising his valour,
   here was the King granting him leave.

In uniform rough as a cat's tongue
   the soldier artlessly said,
'Hard are the stones on the Eastern Front,
   but, Sire, harder at home is my bed.'

Though flagons and goat-meat were offered
   the Hittite refused to go home.
He lingered outside the Palace gates,
   big eyes as dark as the tomb.

Silk merchants came and departed,
    they turned from Uriah appalled –
for the soldier sobbed in the stony heat,
    ignored his wife when she called;

sat down with his sacks, sat in the sun,
    sat under stars and would not quit,
scowled at the King accusingly
    till the King got fed up with it.

'Stubborn Uriah, what do you want?
    Land? Gold? Speak and I'll comply.'
Then two vultures creaked overhead
    to brighten the Hittite's eye.

'Death.' That's what he sought in the desert
    near some nameless stony track.
And there two vultures ate the soldier
    with a dagger in his back.

The widow was brought to the Palace,
    a Queen for the King-size bed,
and oh their teeth like milk were white,
    and their mouths like wine were red.

V

Should there be merriment at a funeral?
Stones of Jerusalem, where is your lament?
Should her face not have been leper-ashen?

Should she not have torn at her apparel
        bayed at the moon?
Is first young love
        always a malady?

When Uriah roared with the Captains of Joab,
        the swearing garrisons,
the dust leaping behind the chariots,
        the wagons, the wheels;
when his sword was unsheathed
amidst the uplifted trumpets
and the cacophony of donkeys:
when he was fierce as a close-up,
        huge with shield and helmet;
when his face was smeared with vermilion,
did she think of him less
        than a scarecrow in a field?

When she was more girl than woman
who built for her
        a house of four pillars?
When his foot was sore
        did she not dip it in oil?
When his fever seemed perilous
        did she not boil the figs?

When the morning stars sang together,
face to face, they sang together.
At night when she shyly stooped
        did he not boldly soar?

When, at midnight, the owl screeched
        who comforted her?
When the unclothed satyr danced
        in moonlight
who raised a handkerchief to her wide eyes?

When the archers practised
        in the green pastures
whose steady arm curled about her waist?

True love is not briefly displayed
like the noon glory of the fig marigold.

Return oh return
pigeons of memory to your homing land.

But the scent was only a guest
        in the orange tree.
The colours faded
        from the ardent flowers
not wishing to outstay their visit.

VI

The wind blows and the page turns over.
    To Bathsheba a babe was born.
Alas, the child would not feed by day,
    by night coughed like a thunderstorm.

'Let there be justice after sunset,'
    cried Nathan, the raging priest.

Once again he cursed the ailing child
  and the women's sobs increased.

So the skeletal baby sickened
  while the King by the cot-side prayed
and the insomniac mother stared
  at a crack in the wall afraid.

Nobody played the psaltery,
  nobody dared the gameboard.
The red heifer and doves were slaughtered.
  A bored soldier cleaned his stained sword.

Courtiers huddled in the courtyard,
  rampant their whisperings of malice.
The concubines strutted their blacks.
  The spider was in the Palace.

Soon a battery of doors in the Palace,
  soon a weird shout, 'The child is dead.'
Then Bathsheba's teeth like milk were white,
  and her eyes like wine were red.

Outside the theatre of the shrine
  David's penitent spirit soared
beyond the trapped stars. He wept. He danced
  the dance of death before the Lord.

That night the King climbed to her bedroom.
  Gently he coaxed the bereaved

and in their shared and naked suffering
the wise child, love, was conceived.

CODA

Over the rocky dorsals of the hills
the pilgrim buses of April arrive,
one by one, into Jerusalem.

There was a jackal on the site
of the Temple
before the Temple was built.

And stones. The stones only.

Are the omina favourable?
Will there be blood on the thorn bush?
Does smoke rising from the rubbish dump
veer to the West or to the East?
So much daylight! So much dust!
This scribe is
and is not
the Scribe who knew the King's spittle.

After the soldier alighted,
a black-bearded, invalid-faced man,
stern as Nathan, head covered,
followed by a fat woman, a tourist
wearing the same Phoenician purple
as once Bathsheba did,

her jewelled wrist, for one moment,
a drizzle of electric.

But no bizarre crowned phantom
will sign the Register
        at the King David Hotel.

Like the lethargic darkness
of 3000 years ago,
once captive, cornered
within the narrow-windowed
        Temple of Solomon,
everything has vanished into the light.

Except the stones. The stones only.

There is a bazaar-loud haggling
        in the chiaroscuro
        of the alleyways,
tongue-gossip in the gravel walks,
even in the oven of the Squares,
a discontinuous, secret weeping
of a husband or wife, belittled and betrayed
behind the shut door of an unrecorded house.

There is a kissing of the stones,
a kneeling on the stones,
        psalmody and hymnody,
winged prayers swarming in the domed hives
of mosques, synagogues, churches,
ebullitions of harsh religion.

– For thou art my lamp, O Lord . . .
– In the name of God, Lord of the Worlds . . .
– Hear the voice of my supplications . . .
– And forgive us our trespasses . . .
– The Lord is my shepherd I shall not want . . .
– My fortress, my high tower, my deliverer . . .
– The Lord is my shepherd I shall not . . .
. . . my buckler, my hiding place . . .
– I am poured out like water . . .
– The Lord is my shepherd . . .
. . . and my bones are vexed . . .
– The Lord is . . .

    – Allah Akbar!
    – Sovereign of the Universe!
    – Our Father in Heaven!
    – Father of Mercies!
    – Shema Yisroael!

There is a tremendous hush in the hills
    above the hills
where the lizard is on the ledges,
where the snake is in the crevices,
after the shadow of an aeroplane
    has hurtled and leapt
below the hills and on to the hills
    that surround Jerusalem.

Just a Moment

As my wife arranges the lilac in a vase
I think how for years I've stared from this window
at that garden tree so stark it seemed ashamed;
or as now in May, proud – dressed to the nines,
rustling its green silks and in stately bloom.

I've stood here observing Time's sorcery,
the petroleum sunset behind its branches,
the midges energetic above the grass,
or the rising moon a phoenix in its high leaves.

I have grown old watching such things
and thought how a poet's late adagios
like those of Beethoven (*Muss es sein?*)
should say more about the seasons of fate
than the years have wings and the hours pass.

But now I'm attentive to the window itself
and, for a moment, I've cracked it again, trespassed
into the half-mad timeless world that is still
where I am not old nor will be older –
the tip of my tongue against the glass,
the chill touch of it, the nothing taste of it,
until I breathe in the jubilant Yes
and mortally precarious fragrance of lilac
my wife has just placed upon the windowsill.

Terrible Angels

One bedtime, my father showed me his war medals,
their pretty coloured ribbons, and told me
the other story about the angels of Mons,
that élite and puissant expedition from God:
how first their invisible presence caused horses
to bolt and flocks of meat-snatching birds to rise,
circle around and around like a carousel.

But war coarsens (he said) even genteel angels.
When they spoke it was the silence of gas, amen;
when they sang it was shrapnel striking helmets;
then, finally, soldiers' prayers and soldiers' screams
thrilled the cold angels to steal the muskets
of the dead, to become stealthily visible,
bold and bloodthirsty, true facsimiles of men.

(My father, invalided home, was told
he knew more about angels than was healthy.)

The Relic

(A variation of Ewald Osers' translation of 'Paradise Lost' by J. Seifert)

I, Jaroslav Seifert,
opened the pages of the bible
and my mother, my expert,
taught me the cognominal codes
of the Old Testament women.

Adah signifies rich ornament;
Ophrah, gentle mare of the red deer;
Abigail, true source of joy
(Come out to play, come out to play);
and Naamah, one whose beauty
could lead the open-mouthed angels astray.

But when, years later, blow after blow,
they dragged away the Jews,
their children scared and helpless,
not one of us dared
to call out a modest 'No'.

Tamar signifies palm tree
with its dates, its sugar and wine;
Zilpah, a little droplet
of such a little drop;
Jemima means peaceful dove, pure and divine;
and Tirzah, pleasure-giving (as in love).

But they dragged away the Jews.
Tallest behind the barbed wire
Jecholiah, half-skeleton, his big eyes
so soon to feed the flies. Such a joke!
His name signifies 'The Lord is All-Powerful'.

Rachel means warm woolly ewe-lamb;
Delilah, ringlets, falling tresses,
their darknesses and their points of light;
Deborah, a swarm of honey bees;
Esther, starbright starbright.

And I almost forgot, Shoshana.
Oh Shoshana means rose,
the only flower left to us on this earth
from the Eden that was.

The Story of Lazarus

After the war he settled in kindly Cardiff
his English uncertain, his Welsh not at all.
For three years a clerk who hardly said a word.

Then, accusingly, he showed us the number
on his arm, spoke of how he had survived
in his chemistry, the sudden sound of
his heartbeat. Each stark detail. We were shocked.

Week after week this man's monstrous story
heard in Whitchurch, Llandaf, Canton, Cathays,
in pubs and clubs – The Three Elms, The Conway,
The Golden Shark, the Post House, the Moat House;
told even to Cardiff's patient statues:
John Batchelor, Lloyd George, Nye Bevan.

We closed our eyes till we, too, became stone.

So he whispered his dark story to our children
and years later to our children's children.

Soon they merely nodded, eager to join
the procession banging its way outside
to the Firework Display above Roath Park,
the oompha, oompha, down the street fading.

My Cousin Sidney, the Soldier

When my cousin, the soldier, returned,
no showers of paper fluttered downwards,
no flags were strung across the street.
At his house no energetic Dalmatian
came bounding out, wagging its tail.
But they say a stranger stepped in front of him
on the front path, took out a key,
and opened the front door. Closed it.

They say my cousin, the soldier, stood still,
observed the front room's surprising curtains;
looked to the right – the neighbour was cutting a hedge,
looked to the left – the traffic lights changed.

I've never believed such stories.
I still don't believe in them.
I remember my cousin, the soldier.
When he was a child he would sleep
with his eyes and mouth wide open like a dead fish.

Prufrock at the Seaside

A beautiful woman should be looking at me
as I think big thoughts and stare at the sea.

On this cliff I feel like a movie star
but without my glasses I can't see far.

Perhaps if I had a little more hair
and owned a Rolls-Royce like a millionaire

those bikini ladies mincing by
would, like greedy bees, to my honey fly.

Once I wore the bottoms of my trousers rolled
but my legs are thin and feel the cold.

'You should have married Maisie,' said her friend,
'personified contentment, love without end.'

Pectoral young men play football on the beach
under circling seagulls crying each to each.

'Maisie sweet,' I'd said, 'marry me' but she turned sour,
looked as cheerful as Schopenhauer.

Afterwards, forever, for the sake of my health
I thought it best to mate with myself.

A small boy throws a stone to skim the sea,
a black dog runs after it uselessly.

I remember the sandwiches my mother made,
my teeth grinding sand, red bucket and spade

and in the car going home we all would sing
'Stormy Weather'. Me as Sinatra or Bing.

The football players' shadows run and grow long.
Suddenly the prom's coloured lamps come on.

Look! That scandalous couple. He's stroking her breast.
Oh King David, voyeur, I see them undressed.

The sundown's punctual, the clouds are dyed.
I'm no Don Juan – but what if I'd tried?

I still dream of Maisie, rose with a thorn,
she a queen to lead me, I her willing pawn.

The waves lash on but the sea's in its chains.
The beach becomes desolate. The dog remains.

The Yellow Bird

I do not want it
the witchcraft song of the yellow bird,
nor this room of whisperings

as the slanting rain punctual
pelts against the windowpane.

I do not want it
the heavy brocaded curtains motionless,
her face in profile, Egyptian-like,
unsmiling, emotionless,
staring into the sorry street.

I do not want it
these mirrors without reflections,
these clothes ritually torn, rage in rags,
this piano-lid closed,
a coffin of music.

They say the yellow bird in anger
can only sing sweetly. Not so.

It sang piercingly
in the garden, at the cool of the day,
when Adam, fearful, hid among the bushes.

It sang raucously,
turning its dreadful, juridic beak
in the ululating caves of the troglodytes.

And it sang eerily
in the courts of Osiris, the sunsetter,
the lord of the dead, the judge of souls.

There are no frontiers, my friend, for the yellow bird.

It sang, hovering above the fire,
its wings beating just above the fire,
before the warriors ate their prisoners.

Later, it sang the glory of the celestial
for St Paul in his trance
to become his pet bird, his ally and harbinger.

It sings still at the River Styx
as the ferry crosses and the dog barks;
and in the evening ghost-mists
of long ago deserted battlefields.

It sings in every hospital at 3 a.m.
the song of incurable darkness.

I do not want it
the four coal-black limousines
now hushing their way
to a crematorium.

I do not want it
the overt horror in the beauty
of the wreath.

I do not want it, I do not want it,
the congregation that dare not weep,
the weariness of the Godman,
his mechanical laudation,
his secret ennui of disbelief.

Sing noiselessly, yellow bird,
if sing you must. Or sleep.

1945, 2001

The Appointment

Since the last place I want to be
is where I'm heading towards
why do I welcome the road signs
which point to that destination?

And since the best I can hope for
is to arrive late, if not later,
why am I pressing down my foot
on the damned accelerator?

Fly

He was talking about Kierkegaard
when I observed a housefly had chosen
to settle on his elegant left shoe.

He was saying how we are a mixture
of the finite and the infinite
unaware of this fly, a masterpiece.

He was saying we are a synthesis
of the temporal and the eternal
while the fly's proboscis sucked his shoe.

And when it crawled on to his exposed sock
I thought how the female domesticus,
programmed, lays its eggs in refuse or dung;

how the larvae, those small white maggots,
change to pupae without casting their skins
till eight days later the perfect fly emerges.

Itzig Takes to Philosophy

When asked what he had learned
at the Adult Evening Class (Philosophy)
Itzig defined 'Felaptron'.

It is a mnemonic, he said,
that represents the fourth mood
in the third syllogistic figure
in which a negative general major premise

and an affirmative general minor premise
yield a negative singular conclusion –

unlike 'Ferison', a mnemonic
that represents the sixth mood
of the third syllogistic figure
in which a negative general major premise
and an affirmative singular minor premise
yield a negative singular conclusion.

Of all this, continued Itzig, I was ignorant
till I joined the Adult Evening Class (Philosophy).

Random Birthday Thoughts

Leaving the pavement to negotiate
revolving doors of the Angel Hotel
I thought of all those millions born (not cloned)
crying, 'I am' the same laboured minute,
and of those going out from this world
as others were coming in – as if, compelled,
they had pushed on God's revolving doors
so some, suffering, could quit more easily.

I thought too, of God's noxious bacteria
which I had seen earlier that morning,

all appearing to be identical
beneath an astonished microscope
like the swart pips of archaic apples,
perdurable detritus of Eden.

And then I thought of how, when I was a boy,
I'd been told to use the word 'unique' rarely
since everything is; and of Abraham
ruining his father's business, wild
with an axe in the prosperous idol shop,
screaming The Lord is One, The Lord is One.

Enemies

Remembering dirty deeds and verbal blows
Heine said he'd be glad to forgive his enemies
once their bodies were swinging on a gallows.

I have an affinity with Heine.
To forgive my enemies is my quest.

But no need for them to swing on gallows
pecked to meat by magpies and by crows.
A Garden of Rest will do – one well-cared
for, well-aired – fragrance of cut grass,
gravel pathways, elaborate headstones.

No expense spared. I'll pay.
(Such charity they say is blessed.)
I'm so longing to be virtuous.
I'm so impatient to pardon them.

Phone Call at Ogmore-by-Sea

At 3 a.m., the hour of the rising Dead,
Hello, Hello? No-one spoke.

Hello? Hello? I wait and know
the intimidation of silence.

                    Discharged
from the lunatic asylum of sleep
now alert, adrenal, I explore
the moonstruck window.

Outside, the sighing, fussy
surge of the sea swarming up
the unpeopled, pebbled shore.

Certain nights the house creaks
and the nearer I move to the dead hour
the smaller I become.

I've eaten my prunes, Daddy.
I've taken my cod-liver oil.

The clock's disarmed.
The night-bird is flying to the moon

and wind and cloud play lighting tricks
above the inebriated-dancing sea
that flaunts mock silver on its blacks.

Religion

Blithely, the stranger on the soapbox claimed
that God was created when they prayed;
that, at night, mystic lights magnified the church,
the abandoned one at the top of the hill.

'Go, at midnight,' he said, 'hear organ music
and ecstatic voices as pure as angels'.'
So they obeyed and climbed the hill of lampposts,
afraid they might find the proof they hoped for.

But the windows were dark and no voices sang.
The doors opened to the muteness of stone
and, relieved, they fell to their knees and prayed.

Song: Yes

Yes to busy music that bullies,
employs your feet, makes you sing;
first love, love that is brief,
shaken-daffodil season,
consummate picture of Spring.

Yes to tra-la-la summer music
pastoral-rich, score unsigned;
sunflower triumphant,
a surprising lit window
before the drawing of a blind.

Yes to grand brooding symphonies
of Berlioz or Mahler;
autumn's fire with chorus,
flowers solemnly dying
in the funeral parlour.

And yes to snow-bleak adagios
that hold the old in thrall
till their chilling pictures fade
unlike the hooks behind
on the white and vacant wall.

So put your arms about your love
as if she were Molly Bloom
and let your seed-cake kisses be
all the seasons' yes of music
and yes and yes beneath the moon.

Summoned

Yesterday you stood inert, spiritless,
at a curtained suburban window.
Two small blackbirds appeared
typing the front garden's grass.
Then a solitary, shabby crow.

You thought how an accompaniment
played on a piano with one finger
could be of great importance,
so why not inharmonious bird-music,
the sweet and the harsh?

Sing birds, you called, sing in unison,
and gently tapped the glass.
They lifted away at once, vanished,
and you carried on with your old life
as if nothing had happened.

Things

Nichts ist mir zu klein, und ich lieb es trotzdem
und mal' es auf Goldgrund und gross . . .
                                    R. M. Rilke

The strange, changing intimacy
of closely examined things
that studious painters know.
Dead caterpillars take wings.

Keepsake pebbles, exiled shells,
looted from some holiday shore,
this mysterious giant key
that opens no familiar door.

So many things not wanted,
so many things outgrown:
a red uncomfortable chair,
an outdated telephone,
a vase in detestable taste
once won at an Easter fair.

A shiny suit, a discarded shoe,
clocks that no longer tick,
a broken musical box –
Frère Jacques, dormez-vous?

So many things finished and old
that make Time visible;
and nothing too useless
or graceless, or diminished
that cannot be tenderly painted
on a background of gold.

Praise May Thither Fly

Let us praise the blaspheming Old Masters
though some in greed lied and cheated,
and some, unsavoury, beat their wives,
or strangely let their wives beat them!

And some, perhaps, once or twice a year
at sundown thought the monstrous shadow following
momentarily was not their own.

All, all sycophants of magic,
all flea bitten, mosquito bitten, lice infested,
smelly practitioners of the absurd
who by indirections found directions out
– this ordinary man, that ordinary man,
one minute a sinner, the next a seer.

Such accidents of craft! Such hauntings!
As if they had heard a robust shout
in the wind –
some believing what they did not hear.

There – at the very centre of the circle
where work becomes worship,
such danger to themselves
when they, half-tranced, amazed themselves

retrieving from the Invisible
(some dared not sign their names)
crazed saints, hovering haloes,

the stout, ruminating Virgin
with her hefty baby, Jesus,

and, leering amongst the attentive angels,
the monstrous one they quickly painted out.

North

Between the black tree trunks
the snow, white as a frightened eye,
and still the snow-shocked road
looped North, always North.

In a stinging panic the disorder
of flying snowflakes resumed,
blown by the wind that howled
and hated us. We looked back

for our footprints but
they no longer followed;
so much blank, ruffled napery
and we seemingly anaesthetised.

The sweat froze on our foreheads
and, suddenly, we saw it
for one sublime moment only,
the white horse in the snowstorm.

Trembling, awake with otherness,
we did not shout at the wind.
Then all was as before. Silently
we tracked North again. Always North.

Heroes

Lightning brings a bullying downpour,
makes people drenched loiter in doorways.
An emptiness drifts through the streets of London
as if there had been news of a pestilence.

And here it comes again, thunder's shrapnel,
the grand formidable squares abandoned
but for the statues of forgotten heroes –
nameless soldiers and their generals on horseback

riding nowhere, thrashed by a serious rain
which seems merciless as they once were
while, in the gutters, the busy water
now is British red, history down the drain.

Piano

At 66 Sandringham Crescent
an upright piano was being eased down
a long flight of stairs by three men
all wearing off-white overalls.
Backward, staccato, two stepped
descending
   one
      stair
        at
          a
            time
till the taller of the two men
began to collapse in slow

slow   slow motion
and the piano
  leapt
    to the hallway's rising floor
crashing its memories of music:
simple tunes such as 3 Blind Mice,
as well as great meaningful sonatas
of profundity and faraway,
into a scattered anarchic jigsaw
of free-loving volatile
meaningless sounds
fading

till the stricken piano
lost its memory entirely.
After the ambulance arrived (too late)
one removal man lit a cigarette

and sensing the wide-awake stare
of the householder

tapped the grey ash, with great delicacy,
to the hollow of his cupped left hand.

Shobo

He hardly knew a single English word
and was too much in pyrexial sloth
to throw 16 kola nuts from his right hand
to his left. The interpreter grumbled
that he worried about your clay-red tie.
This colour, it seemed, invoked the wrath
of Shopanna, Lord of the Open Spaces.

You were not trusted. You knew nothing of
his gods, their shrines, those tall pillars of mud,
nor of the dread power of the earth-spirits.
He felt himself to be perversely cursed
and could not send for the babalawo
– the priest who kept water in his house
but preferred, sometimes, to bathe in blood.

You were too rational in your white coat,
unable to offer analgesic words
in the right order. And no heaven-sent

antibiotic could dispatch a curse.
So away he wasted, eyes ever more distant.
Pyrexia of unknown origin, you said.
He died. Status lymphaticus, you said.

And the post-mortem revealed little cause.
A thymic death? Guilt and his fey belief
in a vile incubus? Sometimes I think
of Shobo at night, mystery's habitat,
where a man may fancy he hears a footfall
on the stairs becoming faint, fainter,
ever more distant, till not heard at all.

Lucky

(for Max)

Lucky, lover of balls, one at her paws,
brown eyes patient, expectant, impatient.
Go on, pick it up you nitwit, she seems to say,
throw this one, bowl it overhead, a googly if you like.

No! I don't want to hear again your story
of the daft sincere girl in the pavilion
who reckoned you're a great bowler
because you hit the bat every time.

And don't drone on about evening sunlight
cloud-shadows chasing a red ball to the boundary,
the ripple of disconnected applause
like money shaken in a charity box.

And don't tell me about the big winter-egg either
prematurely flying towards the tall H.
Just pick this one up, this one, yeh, and
forget the soccer ball which your left foot
squinted the wrong side of the post.

And don't even think about
those upper-class wooden guys on horseback
who thwack their hockey sticks
at a round apology of a thing
you can't even get your teeth into.

And definitely, definitely, disremember
the golf ball that with your usual help
arced and vanished into legend,
sniffed out, you'd probably have it,
by that blind, clever-dick, clapped-out Argus

while Penelope's noisy claque
jumped and jostled for a beach ball,
and those delicate Phaeacian damsels
played catch to the sound of music.

Book stuff! Give it a rest, old nitwit.
Just throw this ball and above all abjure the one

that you, with such a haunted, insomniac look,
hurl too often through the gone years
to where I, Lucky, can't run and run,
tail Time-wagging, to proudly bring it back.

Iolo Morganwg

I, Ellis Owen, antiquary and stone epitaph versifier,
testify this morning of February 29th, 1856,
that at Madam Totti's Wednesday night seance
widow Gweneth Jones, scrubber of germs and humbug,
dared to ask in the tricks and shivers of candlelight,
'Where are you now, you rogue, Iolo Morganwg?'

What a shuffling silence! No disordered valediction
from the best poet ever to have languished
in Cardiff Gaol; no protesting squeak at all
from our druid-conceiver, our most loud tremendous liar
for whom each Bristol Channel porpoise became a whale;
no Welsh Red Indian curses – not a single scoffing word
from Iolo who faked and forged great Dafydd's verses
– he transcribed one, then invented seven –

until we heard his alto voice, sweet as syrup, saying,
'My dear Mrs Jones, my sugar lump, my hazelnut,
here I am, my old snowdrop. Here in Heaven.'

Ovid's Wish

I'd rather be in hell with one woman
than in heaven with all those sexless angels.

Corinna may deceive me and then we
quarrel — but oh what reconciliations!

True, Desire's lantern burns dimly sometimes
yet with a little oil it soon flares up.

You know how it is: a horse bolts suddenly
and, helpless, the rider tugs at the reins.

Or a yacht is driven back from the shore
when its bold sails are caught in gusts of wind.

Well, Cupid's arrows know their own way home.
They feel more at home in me than in their quiver!

Life's on lease. Why settle for eight hours' sleep
and ignore delightful flighty Cupid?

Sleep's a rehearsal for undying Death.
There's time enough for nights of peace. So shoot

on, with one eye closed, mischievous boy:
let your arrows seek my heart for ever.

The Jeweller

That rainy night, the Poetry Reading over, he drove me home.
'As a doctor you must have seen many a bloody sight,
– but you poets no longer delight in the serenity of things.
If you had my job would you write of jewels fit for kings:
the delicate yellow-tinted topaz of Brazil, maybe,
or the wine-hued topaz sometimes set in queenly rings?'

Then I, at the traffic lights, saw the joy of stealthy colours
on the black wet tarmac. (First you see them, then you don't.)
Not the terminal jaundice in Freda's eyes, nor the wings
of rosacea on Goronwy's face, but the gold alloy
tiara that Clytemnestra wore at Delphi
and the heart-stopping rubies Agamemnon stole from Troy.

Dylan

(*At the Poetry Library, London, 9th November 2003*)

I put down my glass of white wine chilled
to unveil his eyeless staring head.
A heard silence. A stone dropped down a well.

Speeches. His lust for the arson of the word;
his impecunious life like water spilled
from a cupped hand; how Fame advanced spotlit,
wearing jewels over her sores; how her pimp
whispered, 'Dilly, Dilly come and be killed.'

A Letter to Stanley Moss in New York

Dear 'Colleague in the art' your invitation
to your son's wedding in Fiesole
arrived on one of those grey pensioner days
when the apple lies worm-eaten in the wooden bowl.
I had awakened to a September day
that would have rusted on a railway siding
and left no visiting card behind.
But now, Fiesole-thoughts irradiate my mind
with an avalanche of jubilant sunlight.

Alas, I can't be with you. I'm committed
to present my lecture on Death at Llanbadarn
for the resurrected Merrie Wales Society.
Hurrah, though, I say whenever two dare to marry.
It's such a brisk signal of optimism, isn't it?
Like Eve saying Au revoir on leaving Paradise.

You write that you've ordered your centaurs
and your Russian dancers to Fiesole.
No father could do more. A price above rubies.
I wish I could send my platoon of corybants
but they outrageously absconded years ago
to the fertility goddess's bunker.
Instead, I offer your son my only advice:
Hilarity is not welcome at the breakfast table.

Also I've penned a note to my agent in Florence
to supply bride and groom with a dozen jars
of my good, deodorized, golden eye-ointment.
I trust this gift will not be misunderstood.
You know how that can be. Our Z and your Z.

The final letter of the alphabet, by the way,
I always think, is on its knees praying
with its back to the abyss. Do you agree?

Meanwhile, I'll post the ecstatic couple
(let their life be all honey and nightingales)
a photostat of my lecture on Death.
Please keep a slice of wedding cake for me.

Politics in the Park

Almost soaring from his soapbox,
frantic, gesticulating, betrothed
to language, he deplored
the paradox of slums and cripples
in a world of colours. And
righteously cursed statesmen
by murder fed, by murder clothed.

There and then I determined
to join the money-box shuffling
party of exile from Yes-man's Land.
I cared, you see, I deeply cared.

Mesmerised by the theatre of his mouth,
I can't recall what else he said.

I can't recapture his North, his South,
and somehow, I never did enrol.

But afterwards I felt so carefree,
so entranced, as I stared
at the highest, jubilant, silver
sunlit point of a fountain.

All Things Bright and Beautiful

Faint, reassuring for some, the bells outside.
This is England. Religion not quite dead!
Besides, a fat daft bee zigzagging this room
(windows open) seems to mumble a Sunday matin
and I recall how my least of religion
and my little Latin have been scrubbed out
like chalk from Brother Vincent's 6th Form blackboard.

Once Sir thrust his Roman beak towards me,
the bleak crucifix above his head.
'You say you never pray, boy? Never?'
All those fustian words by rote. Affluent beggars
falling to their knees in the gloom of a church
and a god in agony upon a wall.
I shambled. Was this the Inquisition?

I would not convert. Fear is the hasp of Religion.
I'd be a hero, write 'amo' in wine
and ignore the Hand no man can grasp.
Let the priest rage, kindle lightning and thunder,
thrash the cane-rod on his long black skirt.
'All I believe in, Brother, is wonder.'

And I thought of the odd idiot boy, Rhys,
on the high Wenallt range, looking down,
suddenly crying out, 'Oh, well done God.'

But now this room is quiet. The bee has blundered
into the garden and soon Religion's bells will cease.

At Caerleon

This shadowy spring evening,
in these ruins of Caerleon,
I hear the alarm of distant shouts.
Soon the skinhead knights
of The Round Table gang appear.
Bored, they horse around, frab,
and throw empty cans of beer
at each other.

The scarred and tattooed
loudest lout

seems to be their King.
The long knife in his buskin
is as keen as Arthur's sword.

Deprived, they bully language
into oaths
until, suddenly, together,
as if a starting gun had sounded,
the outcast, broiling yobs depart
to seek another gang to cull.

A smear of blood on a silken flag,
a golden crown on a decaying skull,
a lust for heroes,
this is where the legends start.
And I'm alone at last,
can lose my reason,
sit upon a stone and play
(paper on a comb) a mournful tune
from an imagined country
that would break an exile's heart,
or summon silhouettes like phantoms
who were coming,
came and now have passed.

On the Coast Road

This ash-end of the year, too short of light,
the grumpy afternoon closes down
and a bossy wind summons, like a conductor,
choirs of ghosts to the telegraph wires.

Soon the roofs of Ogmore recede out of sight
as I walk on awake in the wrong weather.
Ahead, a seagull squeals, bullied off course,
and sheep scrum behind stone-armoured walls.

Tons of air! And nobody on this coast road,
and nobody on the beach below where
the thaumaturge sea thrashes the rocks
and hey-hey presto, fakes fountains of snow.

Down there, on that rock's pulpit, my father fished
till his own days grew shorter. Now, briefly,
this road leads to the Past. Is it the scolding wind
that makes my teeth ache and my eyes water?

At the old, shut farmhouse, I meet a boozy gang
in fancy dress. The man in a white sheet
holds up, on a pole, the skull of a horse.
The Mari Lwyd! I blink. They vanish of course

and the graffito I, as a boy, once chalked
on the ruined barn beyond this farmhouse
has vanished too: STRAIGHT ON FOR THE FUTURE.
Quick, bird, quick, present winds shake the lamp-posts

into staring light. As if pursued, a tin can
buckets past me, scrapes the bleak macadam,
its off-key tinkle diminishing plaintively
with each forward struggling step I take.

At the Concert

Only yesterday while walking on Ogmore cliffs
one listless sheep gave me the yellow eye.
Its jaws moved sideways, munching over and over.
The same old grass. Same old flavour.

I strolled inland and saw the big brown horse
in Lol's sloping field. It stood utterly still.
When I returned it hadn't moved an inch.
It must have been as bored as any statue.

And here's a pretty Miss next to me, motionless.
She'll sit in Row G unawakened by
the conductor's sudden convulsions till
the very last note like a Prince's kiss.

And how's your life? Static too? Do you wait,
as I do, numb, for something to happen
until it happens? If so, join the queue.
It stretches all the way to the Old People's Home.

I'm thinking all this, I mean about the sheep
and the horse, about you and about me
as I pretend to listen to Klump's new free-form
yawn-fecund 'Machine of Dissonances'.

What else can I do except try not to cough
while my cat back home squats in my chair
unmolested, deigning to blink now and then
at the soundless blank TV screen? I wish

I were there, staring through the garden window
at the pear tree in its serene magnificence –
an April epiphany. No wonder, here, now,
Miss is clapping too and someone shouts, 'Bravo'.

A Marriage

Love, almost three score licit years have passed
(racist fools said our marriage would not last)
since our student days, honeysuckle nights,
when you'd open the jammed sashed window
above the dark basement flat and I, below,
would be an urgent, athletic Romeo.

Remember when I hacked my shin and swore
and you put an exclamation mark to your lips
because of the German landlady's law

NO VISITORS AFTER 10 P.M.
She kept castrating instruments for men!

Up the creaking stairs Indian file, the door
closed, you'd play before one amorous word
a Louis Armstrong record or another diverting disc
lest something of our nothings would be heard.

Oh the stealth of my burglar's exit through the dark,
the landlady's dog, that we called Wagner
alert, anti-Semitic, lifting its ears
to rehearse a virtuoso chilling bark.

I hear its echo still at the front garden gate,
down the lamplit street, faint, through the hurrying years
to where we are, in sickness and in health,
in perdurable love, ageing together,
lagging somewhat, slowly running late.

2004

The Malham Bird

(For Joan)

That long summer a clarity of marvels
yet no morning News announced the great world
had been reinvented and we were new,
in love – you a Gentile and I a Jew!

Dear wife, remember our first illicit
holiday, the rented room, the hidden beach
in Wales, the tame seagull that seemed a portent,
a love message, as if Dafydd's ghost had sent it?

After our swim we lay on our shadows naked,
more than together, and saw high in the blue
two chalk lines kiss and slowly disappear.
Then the friendly gull swooped down, magnified, near.

Now, three grandchildren later, I think of
a black feathered bird, the malham of Eden,
how it took advice, closed its eyes resolute,
when others singing pecked forbidden fruit;

and how, of all the birds, it was not banished
but stayed, lonely, immortal, forever winging
over the vanished gardens of Paradise.

With Compliments

Dear, if I had a small legacy from Croesus
I would purchase – please do not argue –
that painting of gladioli by Soutine
you so admired. But in a waking fit
of realism I've bought
this bunch of robust-red,
radiantly alive upstanding gladioli
from The Corner Flower Stall instead.

First Baby

No angel disguised as a beggar
in the brevity of a mirage
knocked on our front door.

The scarecrow did not speak,
the foxes of midnight did not bark.
No commotion of the wind.

No V-patterned squadron of swans
in their wedding gear flew over,
but we have a new birthday to mark.

Welcome daughter. Welcome, unconfined!
This is your homecoming.

Your little hands grope the air.
Your pupils are nuances of blue
and remnants of Nothing.
You cry and suddenly the world is old.

A shadow bends over you,
a silhouette hugs you close.

It's party time.
Bring in the excellent dancers.
With a hey and a ho
pipe on those oaten straws.

It was you, baby, that was crowned.
Now your mother is.

Bring in the flowers like compliments.
It's her royal right.

She's a benign victorious empress
and we her awe-struck servants.
Her bed's a burnished throne,
your cot's her jewel box.

What's new, baby?

Sloppy Love Poem

'Enough amorous hyperboles,'
Catullus to his lover said.
'Let's kiss 1000 times
and after, count 1000 more.'
They untangled quickly
to undress for bed.

But one loose kiss or two
undid their duff agenda
for in their douce and moaning
dovecot they hardly knew
who was who or who was what
and forgot to count the number.

As sly deft Catullus was
so I'm dizzy-daft with you
guilty of lovers' word abuse,
wet confectionery rot: 'muse-baby',
'honey-bunny', 'sweetie-pie', 'pumpkin',
'pet', 'pudding', 'darling apricot'.

Yes, you're the world's 8th dishy
wonder and I love you, pussy cat.
Let owlish professors hoot, 'Tu-who',
it's true, it's true, it's true.
Come angel-face, ginger eyes,
juicy Joan, let's grease the pot.

A Doctor's Love Song

Since I'm heliotropic you must be my sun.
7 times by 7 times I fall at your feet.
You sulk, you smile, you're bitter-sweet.
I'm enthralled. Love, am I a fool of love?

When you're faraway I'm cold,
when you're near I almost scald.
Cynics reckon love's an illness.
Do I need a linctus?
Should I swallow bromides or a tonic?

Love's clown rules the world
not least the tides of marriage.
Listen to my heartbeat. Mitral-like it murmurs
and your cognomen is called.

I've all the signs and symptoms:
pyrexia of well-known origin,
bed-talk intimate and moronic,
loss of commonsense and blithely
certain my ailment's chronic.

Phew! Such hormonal alchemy
I feel so swimmingly alive.
Such side-effects, why panic?
I sway, I foam, I fizz,
like the top of the wave it is.
I breast-stroke and I dive.

Happily I'm legless, breathless, helpless,
and know no remedy to prescribe
till Death himself, marble-eyed,
comes home again to Arcady.

Domestic, 3 a.m.

> *Where the apple reddens*
> *Never pry*
> *Lest we lose our Edens*
> *Eve and I.*
> Robert Browning

You need not be cross, why are you
cross-examining me?

By Ishara, queen of the oaths,
hear me out.
      – Let's contend no more love –

By Ishtar of Nineveh,
by Ishtar of Hatterina
     – do not shout;
what so wild as words are? –

By the fat hypertensive lord of wars,
by St Francis's cat and Santa Claus,
by Gog and Magog and Eskimo Nell,

I, on quitting the flat of Mel and Priscilla,
was caught in the cage of a bloody lift
rattling its bars like a bloody gorilla
and ringing the bloody emergency bell.

I could have been there till Hogmanay.
    – Stop staring at me like that.
By the black pigeons of Dodena,
I could have been there till doomsday –

Please

I'll hoist the white flag high,
I'll blow the bugle of retreat,
I'm already on my knees,
I'll fall 7 times before your feet.
What else, my darling, can I say
except I'm starving and I love you?
OK . . . OK?

A Scene from Married Life

That unseasonable July in Ogmore
nothing was happening until it happened,
the commuters trapped in their stuffy office block,
the sea slow, the Monday beach sullen, empty,

and I, thinking of the squabble with my wife:
fast barbed words that made the other squirm
and fed flushed indignation, verbal revenge –
a dead bird eaten by the early worm.

I piled up my usual clothes and daps tidily
on a convenient boulder brooding nearby
and, troubled, saw the far dank confusion of
the sea and sky in resentful wedlock.

A mile out the monstrous Tusker Rock crammed
with ghosts and psychopomps raised black fangs.
So many boats it had torn asunder. Seagulls
drifted above it like lost thoughts of the damned.

Soon, daring the fussy sea, I entered
a B movie to enact my great climactic scene.
(After I sank – weep for me – the credits would come up,
then the screen, appropriately, would go blank.)

I swivelled for a last winsome longshot, saw
on the high cliff my wife dressed in blue and all
the best of the world true and desirable.
With surrendering waves I crawled to the shore.

Our own cold wars during the real Cold War
were few and brief. Sulky, I'd linger at my desk
but children's cries were mightier than the pen.
And sweet the armistice, each kiss, and then . . .

Yesterday's Tiff

You were ready to boil at 0°.
I wasn't sulking. Simply I thought
no more figs and honey for you,

no more ginger to match your eyes.
Exit Poussin. 'Bye Kandinsky.
Through the window, wham!

You like rum. Down the drain with it.
Raspberries? I've eaten them all.
Go to bed with Ruskin!

That dinner party you plan.
I'll invite Kingsley
and other right-wing boring guests.

A war-monger or two. Do you get
the drift of what I'm saying?
Definitely no more freesias.

Only things that keep you awake
at night: shuffling mice, coffee,
and now, please, me too, silly.

Lachrymae

(i) *The Accident*

I crawled from the noise of the upturned car
and the silence in the dark began to grow.
I called out her name again and again
to where neither words nor love could go.

(ii) *Later*

I went to her funeral.
I cried.
I went home that was not home.

What happened cannot keep.
Already there's a perceptible change of light.
Put out that light. Shades
lengthen in the losing sun.
She is everywhere and nowhere
now that I am less than one.

Most days leave no visiting cards behind
and still consoling letters make me weep.
I must wait for pigeon memory
to fly away, come back changed
to inhabit aching somnolence
and disguising sleep.

(iii) *Winter*

What is more intimate
than a lover's demure whisper?
Like the moment before Klimt's *The Kiss*.

What more conspiratorial
than two people in love?

So it was all our eager summers
but now the yellow leaf has fallen
and the old rooted happiness
plucked out. Must I rejoice when
teardrops on a wire turn to ice?

Last night, lying in bed,
I remembered how, pensioners both,
before sleep, winter come,
your warm foot suddenly
would console my cold one.

(iv) *Swan Song*

Night fuzzy fairground music
and, like kids, we sat astride
daft horses bouncing on
the lit-wide Merry-Go-Round
to swagger away, serene,
old lovers hand in hand.

Now, solemn, I watch
the spellbound moon again,
its unfocused clone drowned
in Hampstead's rush-dark pond
where a lone swan sings
without a sound.

2005

Postcard to His Wife

Wish you were here. It's a calm summer's day
and the dulcamara of memory
is not enough. I confess without you
I know the impoverishment of self
and the Venus de Milo is only stone

So come home. The bed's too big! Make excuses.
Hint we are agents in an obscure drama
and must go North to climb 2000 feet
up the cliffs of Craig y Llyn to read
some cryptic message on the face of a rock.

Anything! But come home. Then we'll motor,
just you, just me, through the dominion
of Silurian cornfields, follow the whim
of twisting narrow lanes where hedges
have wild business with roses and clematis.

Or we could saunter to the hunkered blonde
sanddunes and, blessed, mimic the old gods
who enacted the happy way to be holy.
Meanwhile, dear, your husband is so uxorious
absence can't make Abse's heart grow fonder.

After the Memorial

Some spoke of her unostentatious beauty:
she, passionate moralist, Truth's sweet secretary.
No-one heard the sobbing of the angels.

Well, I have my own weeping to do.
(If angels could weep they would become human.)
I lived her life and she lived mine –
not only in the easy valleys of Pretend
where bosky paths descend to lakes where no swan
is singular (and fish ignore the hunched Angler)

but here where the uphill road to happiness
has ordinary speed limits,
and still the revelation is
that there can be such a thing

until it must yield to a dead end.

So now our marriage book is drowned
(there seemed magic in it)
and she is both manifest and concealed –
manifest because I see her everywhere,
concealed because she is nowhere to be found.

Portrait of an Old Poet

(To Graham Kershaw)

Does the future slyly haunt all portraits,
a preternatural unveiling? It's as if
you saw me, a man grieving who would know
his dear one turned to stone on the M4.

For you caught me there sitting downcast
with arms folded, commanded to do so
by some strange authority – the white
balloon of happiness out of sight.

Sometimes children mime gargoyle-grim
faces in the mirror. The old don't have to!
But till that night when Death divorced us
I'd been nearly as happy as possible.

So I wish you'd painted in the white balloon
we chased after, that I'd pursue still
though it floats up far, smaller and smaller
into the blue and once upon a time.

The Revisit

This scene too beautiful, it seemed a fake:
the sunset sky, the drowning sunset lake.
With you by my side, did I dream awake?

God's spacious canvases always amaze
even when lucid colours become uncertain greys.
There was nothing else we could do but praise.

Yet darkness, like dread, lay within the scene
and you said, 'Just like music that seems serene.'
(Mozart stared at green till he became the green.)

And there, above the lake, of course unsigned,
its surface hoofed with colour by the wind,
were great windows between clouds, fires behind,

as if from Angel wars. Such April bloodshed!
The wide sky-fires flared and their glitter-red
sparks cooled to scattered stars instead.

Now I, bereaved, like the bruised sky in disrepair,
a shadow by my side, hear a far owl's thin despair.
I stare at colour till I am the stare.

The gradual distance between two stars is night.
Ago, love, we made love till dark was bright.
Now without you dark is darker still and infinite.

Magnolia

A happening, a green place, a door slamming,
an almost empty restaurant at night,
a perfume perhaps, anything may provoke
a dormant picture at the back of the mind
to awaken and advance and remind.

So she is with me in the light and dark.

A sunbeam coming and going suddenly
in a quiet room. Always suddenly.
Musical notes from the open window
of a passing car's radio, maybe.

Each day is remembrance day, adagio,
for the new widower and widow.

Their memories. I know, all begin with We.

In the walled garden of Golders Hill Park
the names of the local unfamous dead
are inscribed on wooden benches
in defiance of the ephemeral. There, now,
among the flowers disguised as colours
in competition with each other, their queen,
a magnolia tree, rules supreme, magnificently.

Memory, father of tears, we sat beneath
it once detained by its audacious efflorescence
that's too quick and too brief. It's nature's

festive haiku, it's a magician's vanishing trick.
Hoopla! First you see it, then it's been!

In serene marital silence we observed
its bridal branches slowly violated,
insolently shamed by a small pilfering wind –
white blossom drifting down as in a dream
without a sound, a trifle blood-stained.

Later, we spoke of transience and of Pierre
Magnol, French botanist of the 17th century,
and how magnolias are named after him
though he's long forgotten, his life wiped clean.

On Parole

Dear, so much shared. Then suddenly, solitary
confinement with the cell door half open,
sentence indefinite. After two years I dared.

You would not have liked or disliked her.
By day her sunlight lively and warming.
At night no lighthouse signalled sweet danger

and I on parole from the prison of mourning
where remembrances recur like a circle
till everything's a blur – every damn thing

a tear-blur, for we'd been utterly darned
together: knew light's secret delight: colour.
You gave me all the light you were

so to embrace another seemed a betrayal.
Not so. How could it be? But next morning
her gold was still gold – my silver, pale tinsel.

Stale, dressed in black again, I blinked at the green,
daunting, unsafe world that indisputably is,
then yours faithfully slouched back to jail.

The Violin Player

Too often now, half somnolent, I would go
like Yeats to a fortunate Lake Isle where
unblemished water-lilies never die,
and no solitary swan floats by
from everlasting to everlasting.

And in the tranquil orchard of this Isle
I'd plunder such paradisial apples
that Cezanne could have painted – apples
no bird would have dared to peck at,
fraudulent but beautiful.

Yes, I would go there rapt, recreant,
and stay there because, sweet, you're not here
till, self-scolded, I would recollect
my scruffy, odorous Uncle Isidore
(surely one of the elect) who played

unsettling, attenuated music
long after a string had snapped,
whose beard bent down to interject,
'Little boy, who needs all the lyric strings?
Is the great world perfect?'

Letters

During an unimportant afternoon,
while an appropriate fuss of rain
patters tearfully on a window pane
(your ashes outside in the Ogmore garden),
I read ink-fading letters from your jammed
desk drawer; the earliest, candid and gauche,
when you were 21 and I was 24.

Then we were dunces of love-talk.
Now others, mellow, summon you to keep
the lonely robin in the garden company.
Bending and rising, bending and rising,
you pull up a serious weed or two,

wearing my patched Harris-tweed coat,
Oxfam-rejected – much too big for you.

Look! You've kept my card from Grau du Roi
where I asked for bread, received a rabbit.
You laughed, explained that I was le
and you were la. Now I read sweet words
I daren't repeat. (You would not want me to.)
In mute distress, my hand is at my throat
till I feel nothing like a scar.

I return the letters to the drawer of dust
and dark and paper-clip. They follow
the motion of our marriage, its yes, its no,
its turning axle and escorting felloe,
the 'I love you' peppered with a quip,
the fervent poetry of love-making,
the sober prose of friendship.

The Presence

Though not sensible I feel we are married still.
After four years survival guilt endures.
I should have said this, could have done that,
and your absent presence has left a weeping scar.
Like a heartbeat, you are indispensable.

Each year, I think, the cries of the dead retreat,
become smaller, small. Now your nearness is far
and sometimes I sense you're hardly there at all.
When in company, when my smiles persist,
your distance briefly is like the furthest star.

It's when I'm most myself, most alone
with all the clamour of my senses dumb,
then, in the confusion of Time's deletion
by Eternity, I welcome you and you return
improbably close, though of course you cannot come.

Postscript

Inexplicable splendour makes a man sing
as much as the pointlessness of things;

and you conceded how sweetly the wide-eyed
disfigured of the world's circus have sung
and the powdered clowns in their darkness sing.

So though late, all too late, is it demeaning
to publish love lyrics about you now?
Bitter to recall that once I pleaded,

Love, read this though it has little meaning
for by reading this you give me meaning.

Talking to Myself

In the mildew of age
all pavements slope uphill

slow slow
towards an exit.

It's late and light allows
the darkest shadow to be born of it.

Courage, the ventriloquist bird cries
(a little god, he is, censor of language)

remember plain Hardy and dandy Yeats
in their inspired wise pre-dotage.

I, old man, in my new timidity,
think how, profligate, I wasted time

– those yawning postponements on rainy days,
those paperhat hours of benign frivolity.

Now Time wastes me and there's hardly time
to fuss for more vascular speech.

The aspen tree trembles as I do
and there are feathers in the wind.

Quick quick
speak, old parrot,
do I not feed you with my life?

The Old Gods

The gods, old as night, don't trouble us.
Poor weeping Venus! Her pubic hairs are grey,
and her magic love girdle has lost its spring.
Neptune wonders where he put his trident.
Mars is gaga – illusory vultures on the wing.

Pluto exhumed, blinks. My kind of world, he thinks.
Kidnapping and rape, like my Front Page exploits
adroitly brutal – but he looks out of sorts when
other unmanned gods shake their heads tut tut,
respond boastingly, boringly anecdotal.

Diana has done a bunk, fearing astronauts.
Saturn, Time on his hands, stares at nothing and
nothing stares back. Glum Bacchus talks *ad nauseam*
of cirrhosis and small bald Cupid, fiddling
with arrows, can't recall which side the heart is.

All the old gods have become enfeebled,
mere playthings for poets. Few, doze or daft,
frolic on Parnassian clover. True, sometimes
summer light dies in a room – but only
a bearded profile in a cloud floats over.

In Highgate Woods

Entering the shuffling hush of tamed
Highgate Woods I recall the insolence
of a Polish poet's search for his own coffin.
He wandered through a vast owl-dark forest,
percussed the bark of 200 trees (he wrote)
and, at last, heard the desired woodnote.
He must have been an explorer of a sort,
death-magnetised as are all explorers.

Fantasy can haunt and bedlam itself
into fact; but I'm too old to copy
that poet's half-serious libretto act.
I observe the choreograph of leaf-fall
and dare not tap upon one lordly tree.
Old poets stay at home to become explorers;
the older they get, the smaller they get
and, relentlessly, the trees grow tall.

Portrait of an Old Doctor

Lover of music more than his textbooks'
arrhythmic prose and dated, almost dangerous
his Conybeare and his Boyd's *Pathology*.
(Notes in the margin by the student he was.)

What was it all about? Blunderbuss drugs
prescribed to ease the patient. And moonbeams.

A composer – a Beethoven, a Smetana –
it seemed, could be deaf but not a doctor.

Too often he'd arrived at the acute bedside
feeling unrehearsed and hesitant before
performance. Those staccatos, those wrong notes,
yet, sometimes, sweet victory. Then Canute's pride.

He had been a confidence man for the patient.
That's how it was in The Theatre of Disease
and, at the final act, he had lifted
his stethoscope to listen as if to Mozart.

Then, silently, relatives and friends filed out.
No applause. None for Hippocrates' art.

Winged Back

Strange the potency of a cheap dance tune
                                Noël Coward

One such winged me back to a different post-code,
to an England that like a translation
almost was, to my muscular days
that were marvellous being ordinary.
365 days, marvellous;

to an England where sweet-rationing ended,
where nature tamely resumed its capture
behind park railings. Few thorns. Fewer thistles;
to *Vivat Regina* and the linseed willow-sound
of Compton and Edrich winning the Ashes.

Elsewhere, Troy always burning. Newspaper stuff.
The recurring decimal of calamity.
Famine. Murder. Pollinating fires.
When they stubbed one out another one flared.
Statesmen lit their cigars from the embers.

They still do. With every enrichment
an injury. They bicker and banquet,
confer and dally, pull on cigars that glow
with blood-light. And all my years,
like the arson of Troy, are elsewhere. Ashes.

Cricket Bat

Reclinate and welded to two gloved hands,
its nervous patting and petting of the crease,
the willow of it, the linseed smell of it,
the long rubbered handle ready for
the shuddering and thrill of a three-spring
slyly leaning winking flagrant leg-glide;

or its skill and pleasure in a kissing shot
through the diving slips, so delicate
so sensual; or its prompt dispatch
of a blatant full-toss. But patience
and the seductive waiting game is all.
So it lusts for the loose one and stonewalls

till, boy, it's up for it, the sex of six,
no longer 45 degrees, but embeamed,
astonishing itself with a head-on sweet
collision – the ball's hung flying silence –
while still upraised, vertical, it salutes
the saluting home pavilion and falls.

Moonbright

Afterwards, late, walking home from hospital,
that December hour too blatantly moonbright
– such an unworldly moon so widely round,
an orifice of scintillating arctic light –
I thought how the effrontery of a similar moon,
a Pirandello moon that could make men howl,
would, in future, bring back the *eidolon*
of you, father, propped high on pillow,
your mouth ajar, your nerveless hand in mine.

At home, feeling hollow, I shamelessly wept
– whether for you or myself I do not know.
Tonight a bracing wind makes my eyes cry
while a cloud dociles an impudent moon
that is and was, and is again, and was.

Men become mortal the night their fathers die.

Sunbright

Sunbright sunbright, you said,
the first time we met in Venice
you, so alive with human light
I was dazzled black;
– like heavy morning curtains
in a sleeping bedroom
suddenly pulled back.

And the first time you undressed,
once more, I, frail-eyed,
undeservedly blessed,
as if it were a holy day,
as if it were yuletide,
and feeling a little drunk,
simply had to look away.

Well, circumspect Henry James
couldn't write *The Turn of the Screw*
till he turned his back on sunbright.
Chair around, just so,
to what was alive, beguiling,
in the Canaletto scene below.

Sweet, all this is true or virtually true.
It's only a poetry-licensed lie
when I rhyme and cheat and wink
and swear I almost need to wear
(muses help me, cross my heart) sunglasses
each time I think of you.

The Summer Frustrations of Dafydd ap Gwilym

(Every day I fall in love I do with one or two)

1.   *Dafydd and the Brecon Deacon's Wife (Storm)*

All that July-long languorous Saturday
I, the swarthy one, fawned for her kisses.
Holiday girls are easy and persuasive I was.
I even praised her husband (as I stroked her bum).
'So big in Brecon. So *very* big in Brecon.'

With that Eminent at home, no adder in sight,
at last, in the dark Ceredigion wood we lay.
Then whoops! Zips of sabbath-scolding light
bullied the heights above Cardigan Bay.
Heaven's furniture shifted. My pretty trembled,
leant on one elbow, eyes improbably white.
Up she rose, no arrow swifter, away, away.

Gentlemen, my feelings I'm sure you understand.
Like trying to open a heavy jammed door
and the damned knob comes away in your hand.
Who alerted the gods to have such fun?
(I curse their fervent stupendous din.)
I suppose you could call it, *Celestial Interruptus,*
with me stiff-o, trousers down, saved from sin.

Too bloody powerful her Brecon husband, mun.

2.   *Dafydd at Llanbadarn*

I don't give a monkey-nut for their prissy talk.
Sunday – forgive me, Lord – is an amiable time
to chase the chaste. After church of course.
But no unburdened smile or sweet kiss ever
from one starched lady of Llanbadarn.
And me, so horny, I can hardly walk.

Give them boils, Lord, since none my needs assuage
– not even she whose nose seems like a chair
for spectacles! I ache. If only one, in luck,
roused me in the heather then Garwy himself

would stagger back envious and awestruck.
Lesbians they must be. Give them pox, Lord, and age.

When, parasolled, they left the church slow-paced
along the gravel pathway, past the grand
shadow of the yew, I winked, I whispered.
Nun-faced they frowned their strait-laced Never!
So I, as true a stud as Garwy, stand
near graves, full of sperm. Oh what a waste!

3. *Dafydd's Night at an English Inn*

The wrong side of the border, at the New Inn
beside river reflections of swans and mallards,
the tidy English gave me wary looks.
One did not. Shapely she was and wanton-eyed,
pretty as Morfudd. Of course I played my cards
as waggishly we enjoyed a flask or two.

At dinner, over candle-light, I dared to ask
with Welsh finesse if she would fork my fish
and eat my meat. Nice? The rest of my menu
I won't recite! She half-smiled. Was that a Yes?
In her tight dress her evident bosom heaved.
Too often the dainty ladies I misconstrue
yet twice a day a clock that's stopped is right.

Later, tavern-dark, moon asleep, I sought
her door. Cold my feet on stone. Outstretched my hand,
a blind man's. I stumbled, crashed, and copper pans
went clamouring on the floor. Bloody dogs began

to bark. (Goodbye one night stand) Out came the English,
East and West, lantern-lit, and half undressed:
voyeurs, snobs, poseurs, shouting Robbers! Robbers!

Unmanned, what could I do but join them?
I screamed Robbers! Robbers! louder than the rest.

4.   *Dafydd's Oath*

Between gloom-burdened sentinel yews
Morfudd has gone to inhabit the habit of a nun,
bolted and locked in Heaven's Waiting Room.

Big laughter in the Inn. Small laughter in the pews.
With jokes and clerihews I'm peevishly mocked
for in the Alun Valley it's headline news.

Others there were and in dandelion weather I worded them.
Few would yield. And the morning after, always,
through the window, I'd see the scarecrow in the field.

Priest, in time, write only Morfudd in my dust.
Now she's starched in nun's gown and I, Ovid's man,
am hired to play the clown for Dyddgu's father.

Still, come what may, my ring on heart, I swear
till North star and South star coalesce
I'll be true to Morfudd . . . Well, more or less.

5. *Letter Not Sent*

Rain again and the jaundiced dandelions
startling the overgrown grass. I miss you, Morfudd,
you with the licit girls of Mary, foreheads hidden,
your husband-hunchback, hell-bent, shouting in his glass house,
and I, staring long at these dragon-tongued logs.

For it's so long since our love's tumult, thumbs up,
rhyme-happy, when every delinquent night
I nightingaled you. What was my word-hoard for
if not for your delight? Merely to look at you
I'd ignite into a fine-glowing ember.
Was it all like a promise made in wine?

Once we made a mansion in the greenwood
but summer's over, dulcet one. I'm moon-shot,
love-lorn, lust-locked, thumbs down, imagining
you listening to God's silent silence
– only the rustle of a nun's gown.

But hear me, love. Without you I'm in motley cloth
without a cause – just a funny bard who plays the clown
for princely money, not for your favours and applause.

The bully clock strikes the hour. The tall yews wait for all.
Now say that I'm yours as scarecrows are lonely;
else goodnight and I will sing and pluck
harp's most secret and deepest string for Dyddgu.

Last Visit of Uncle Isidore

No more magic tricks from Uncle Isidore.
The rain-dishevelled roses in their extremity
could have guessed the party was over.
Indoors, long past tea-time, Great Uncle Isidore,
distant relative not always distant,
stayed and stayed. So did the visiting rain.

Mama always said, 'Poor Isidore.' And he was poor.
Wearing my father's old clothes Uncle creaked 'Ouch'
and cursed Arthritis.
    'Not fair. People should suffer
their illnesses when they're young and healthy.'

My elder brother slammed the front door goodbye.
The raincoat-smelling bus would take him
to Tonypandy where the miners assembled
to jeer Oswald Mosley and the police.
    'Uncle Isidore, work?'
my brother had said, 'For decades he did nothing
and he didn't even do that till after lunch.'

For one year Uncle played a violin
for the silent pictures at the Coronet Cinema.
Then he retired.
    'At the same age as Jesus
when he was crucified,' he half-boasted.

Mama left for the kettle in the kitchen.
Uncle, in the armchair, muttered 'I don't feel well.'
He seemed to fall asleep with his eyes open,

staring at nothing, and his face became
a forgery of itself. Was this one of his tricks?

I wanted to go out, play with Philip Griffiths.
At the window I whispered,

> 'Rain, rain go to Spain,
> Come again another day.'

Bluebells

Cycling for the bluebells near St Mellons
two boys tasted the decomposing of the light
in a high echoing tunnel. They stopped,
left foot on the pedal, right foot on the ground,
to lark loudly, My hen Glad is sad aye!

When Keith shouted I DON'T BELIEVE IN GOD
believe in God.. in God.. in God a sudden WHOOSH replied.
   Four pupils dilated.
Tachycardia. A goods train clumped over
and multitudinous thunderbolts shrivelled.

Later, bikes angled against a stout tree,
they heard a meandering bee shopping among the profusion of
   flowers they bent
to pick. Keith said, Devout little bugger.
Sounds like a daft insect's prayer to me.

Through the returning dark tunnel they hurled
echoes and laughed. But the small dot remained
below the big question mark when they came out
(bluebells alive in the handlebar baskets)
blessed in the unanswering light of the world.

Scent

Lately, going in and out of the house
we once shared, I sometimes think
that the dead have many disguises;
so I hesitate at the blue-painted gatepost
– there where the evening midges dance –
because of the propinquity of a twining shrub
you long ago planted – now in jubilating flower
and surrendering faintly
its button-holding scent – one so alluring,
so delinquent, it could have made Adam
fall on Eve, with delight, in Eden.

In this world the scent could have haunted
the sacred gardens of Athens
to distract a philosopher from his thoughts,
or wafted through an open window
of the Great Library in Alexandria
unbidden, prompting a scholar
to uplift his eyes from his scroll.

But what do I care about that.
For me, now, you are its sole tenant.
Compelled I linger, allowing myself
the charm and freedom of inebriating fancy
till the scent becomes only the scent itself
returning, and I, at the gate, like Orpheus,
sober, alone, and a little wretched.

2012

The Bus

Llantwit Major to Bridgend

At the gnat-employed sundown, all shadows long,
the last bus of the summer day bestirred,
then laboured away from Llantwit Major
without one passenger towards the sheepfields.

At each approaching bus stop on the coast road
no-one waited, not even at Marcross's presbyterian-grey
Post-Office shop. Undeterred, the bus, zestful,
passed low dry-stone walls, high hedges, stonecrop.

After St Bride's, a postcard view: to the West
the unrestful sway of the sea, its water-light
stretching beyond the wreck-loving Tusker Rock
to a soul-feast of horizon colour.

But no expectant traveller at Ogmore
hailed the driver – only a fuss of sheep
on the crepuscular road. There, the bus idled
before blustering on to Bridgend's bus station.

Bridgend to Llantwit Major

After a mug of sweet tea and a fag
the driver backed the bus out of its dolorous
berth, steered it into the incurious
busy mainstreet and lamplit dusk of the town.

Three brisk miles, then another three miles.
Still not one man, not one woman boarded
the bus. The sea had begun its night shift,
the great night was spawning its stars.

The driver, proud of his bus, felt depressed.
Nobody. Why? It was demeaning. Back and fore,
what was the point of it all unless
the journey exploded into meaning?

He drove inland with serious celerity
passed familiar oncoming hedges.
On schedule, at the terminus of Llantwit,
the bus arrived empty, yet terrific with light.

Parrotscold

This night in your ordinary unhappiness
dine alone at L'artista not because of the fussy
authoritarian Emperor of Habit. You're timid,
you know the tiredness of doing nothing,

and your old age is chilled with prudence.
Are there also amyloid moths in your memory?
It's your anniversary, stupid. Isn't her name writ
more in your blood than on bloodless stone?

You say, Every day is our anniversary. Maybe,
but tonight forget to finger-fumble your small
world's wounds. Praise instead your dead ally,
your tactful guide, your Beatrice unsurpassed

who for sweet pampered decades shared your bed
and board. (Think! Dante only saw his Beatrice
twice). Now, mast broken, lone helmless years pass
and stone too may crumble. Nothing lasts except

nothing; yet though Beatrice is no more and nothing,
Beatrice is, her shadow hidden in the shade.
So this nightfall, with all your debts to her
unpaid, raise high and higher the full red glass.

A Story

Dear one, tell me a story of elsewhere,
a story young from times of old
when the bees of Hybla were hushed
in the perfumed air – and did not sting.

Tell me a story of honeyed intent,
of a door that was opened slowly for
the improbable Angel of Happiness
but only a beggar was there

and the olive leaves behind him shaken
for nothing in the world was still
till the door was closed, the wine-glass filled,
and the empty chair at the table taken.

In Black Ink

(*Anniversary poem for Leo*)

Seen through a tear the world's a blur.
No rainbow on an eyelash.

It was the morning of the black tie
– no confident peacock strut.
Mourners under dark umbrellas.

Yit-ga-dal ve-yit-ka-dash . . .

In the house behind shut gates
the sadness of unused things.
All was grievous-grey, all was plain
as the stony tablets of the law;
and I thought how I used to scold you
for your peacock's display on Budget Day,
how then, mischievous, you'd scald me,
'You're so bourgeois, so tame. Be bold,
pitch your tent beneath Vesuvius.'

Once together by Roath Park Lake,
at the slow-motion sunset hour,
we both were blessed and dressed in colour.
Dear brother, MP for Happiness,
master-politician, what an elative time
to recite the gospel of the secular!

Later, to those dispossessed, defeated,
in doldrums or in perdition,
you'd render all the light you were.

Now you've been dead three war-scoured years
and your Joseph coat's in rags. The sun's
retreated. Winter weather. And I recall
the sour chant of Hebrew prayer.

Yit-ga-dal ve-yit-ka-dash . . .

'Stubborn', you said. 'I had to be stubborn
to pass each Bill.' Back home ex-miners
sang in hunger, 'Bread of Heaven'.

Outrageous One, I write these lines for you
in modest ink, with fraternal love,
and hear the mocking laughter of the dead.
You wink, you sigh, 'Use a peacock's feather.'

The Girl in the Kitchen

(Evan Walters, 1938)

1

The key's been turned, the kitchen door's ajar.
In the secrecy of silence she who calls me 'sir'
does not know I'm here, watching her,
a licensed voyeur, watching her –
only a shout away and yet so far.

She vexes me. She's unsure, rough, and humble,
but dare I clear my throat, discreetly cough,
enter the bright instant? Or close the door
quietly, turn the key? I have seen enough.
On the canvas I shall possess her double.

2

I do 'oover, I do dust, I do make
the coal-grate glow. When I'm on my knees to scrub
sir stares at my be'ind as if it were

a firebomb. I know them artists. Each one's
a bloody peeping Tom. I don't mind.

I look into a soap-bubble and see us wed;
me with a fag, sir with a cigar. I'd still
prepare 'is food, stitchin' to mend, but I'd drive
'is car. 'E'd paint me nude. I'd be a star –
'is pitcher called, 'Beauty in the kitchen'.

Both Eyes Open

When one shuts one eye one does not hear everything
Swiss Proverb

The tall painter has painted the small painter
in front of his easel. With one eye shut he sees
a landscape after refreshments of rain.
Pearls on grass blades. Nature's jewellery shop.

Look closer. Beneath a mirror of a tree
a girl just visible in a dark skirt.
It must be that both painters love reticence
else her skirt would be a fiery yellow.

In this world that's a mirror of the world
the tall painter paints for the small painter
a bird in the tree that cannot be seen
and a girl in a skirt he'd rather not see.

I'm coming to think that this painted world
is a familiar — one visited within a mirror
or more likely dreamed about, both eyes open,
where I walked through gateways to that other world.

Listen! the girl in a fiery yellow skirt
is entranced by the singing bird hidden in the tree
which neither of the painters painted.
I wait for it to fly out of the frame.

Blue Song

Some things there always are,
Eros in the end must lose.
Picasso paints a guitar,
that way he sings the Blues.

Henri Matisse harvests colour
more Tangiers than Toulouse.
He says, 'Work can cure everything' —
a prescription to quell the Blues.

Russian cows jump over the moon
(very strong is Russian booze)
but Chagall's cow never lands,
otherwise he'd sing the Blues.

O'Keefe paints flowers in close-up
and critics look for Freudian clues.
Female genitalia. Voyeur!
No wonder the lady sings the Blues.

Is that a telephone or a lobster?
Surely Salvador is confused.
He says, Dial the phone and hear
the lobster trying to sing the Blues.

Rothko squares a mirror with blood
(there's blood in his every bruise),
paints his own reflection out
and soundlessly sings the Blues.

Pale moon-faced Francis Bacon
eerily shrieks and spews
humanoid freaks into a cage.
Odd way to sing the Blues.

Body-detective Lucian Freud
magnifies his sexless nudes
– the uglier the better.
That's how he sings the Blues.

The aloneness of the artist!
So Hockney paints his trees in twos
and Time, itself, in colours passing.
A covert way to sing the Blues.

Damian likes his sheep well-pickled,
I prefer my meat in stews.
Let collectors shed their millions.
Soon they'll sing the Blues.

Is Tracey Emin's messy bed
pertinent British art? J'accuse.
Not for sexpence would I sleep in it
to stop her bawling out her Blues.

Don't speak of artists' rivalry
or their delight in painting nudes,
though every time Pablo scored
Henri sang the Blues.

Do I wish to be a painter
acclaimed with buffs' reviews?
All I lack is talent,
that's why I sing the Blues.

Perspectives

(5 paragraphs for Frank O'Hara)

I sit in L'artista, our local Italian restaurant.
Outside, a rain-thrashed queue waits for their bus.
At an adjacent table, a man with liquorice hair
is shouting to himself; but soon I discover

he's phoning someone. At 1.50 p.m. I order
Fusilli all' Ortolana and their house-red poison.

A waitress bending forward to pick up a spoon
bothers me in more ways than two.
She moves with such grace and femininity
the very earth is richer where she stands.
It surely makes all the clientele forget
their 'nostalgia for the infinite' and to understand,
perhaps for the first time, 'the nostalgia of the infinite'.

Umbrellas pass by the window as I eat my pasta.
Some of it spills onto my trousers, dammit.
Why does this make me think how those poets
who write enigmatic nonsense become famously
the darlings of the professors they most despise?

At 2.23 p.m. I drink my cappuccino and glance
at the TV that's flitting behind the counter.
The 2012 dogs of war are pissing on the dead, Frank.
It could be Syria. Could be Afghanistan.

At 2.40 p.m. the Renoir beautiful one
brings me the bill (£15.10p). She squawks. Pity
her voice like a very active yak makes me shiver.
Outside the rain's gone North. A 2.41 droplet
of pure silver falls from a high tin roof.

Pre-Xmas at L'artista

Sorcery of music! Listening to it some, as in sleep,
become inexact imitations of themselves.
Others, also out of Time, return into another.

When the ugliest beggar you ever saw,
an old soldier's ribbon across his chest,
limped into L'artista, evidently knackered,
to sing Silent Night with such uncanny rapture
the woman at the corner-table, beneath the balloons,
baring her left breast for her baby
began to resemble the brooding figure
in Giorgione's *Tempesta*; our seductive
waitress became a shy Botticelli angel;
L'artista's elegant boss framed in the doorway
posed like the Grand Doge in Gritti's portrait;
and at the long scheming table
a Xmas staff party, no longer rowdy,
seemed ready to model for *The Last Supper*.

The crippled beggar collected his silver
and I thought how beautiful an ugly man can be.
When he opened the door to the outside world
no cool draught was felt from a great beating wing.

Simply, the resident TV resumed its appalling
dominance with scenes of the most debauched,
most up-to-date massacre of the innocents
with haggard Rachel weeping for her children.

A Fan

Too many flaws: my poem less fresh than tinned
but he was one who would never let me fail.
His first sedative gust of praise turned
into an imperious fountain, would not pause,
he pointing out nuances I didn't intend
and I smiled Cheese until I became stale
and I thought of luminous William Blake
enthusing, '*That* is sheer genius,'
and Constable replying, 'Gosh, and there's me
thinking it was only a painting.'

Vignette: High Street after Rain

Sun, suddenly, leaps through, hoopla!
and outside the jewellery shop,
in bravado opposition,
riots of electric raindrops,
hanging from a wire, switch on.

A settled rain pool on the pavement
in slow slow-motion seems to drink
itself up, shrinks, already forgets
the joyous ejaculations of the storm,
will leave behind only its shadow.

Near the pharmacy, the two washed trees
in their best new green, so feminine,

whose gossipy branches interlock, nod
to discuss their rain-pricked leaf-shock
and the Pathetic Fallacy!

Now ladder-high above the rooftops
tantrums of seagulls appear
so soon to disappear,
their wings becoming ever more tiny
like handkerchiefs waving goodbye.

Wasp

At 3 p.m. I'm sitting in L'artista
as usual, bored, waiting for something unusual.
London's under the weather, has become prose.
Don't tell me I should be in the country
watching hypnotised animals standing
motionless in the gloom of an afternoon.

Here, at least, I'm entertained by a wasp:
it hovers near the windowsill's waxen flowers;
deluded, it dives for nectar. Afterwards in anger,
the wasp that does not know it's a wasp
becomes a little, loud, nazi insect-official.
Oblivious, in come two Jewish beards.

Next to my table they seem to discuss Theology
– much concern about the state of a soul –
but soon, like the wasp, I twig I'm deceived
when one takes his boot off to prove his point.
Then the other remarks, 'Well, the heel's all right.'

Look! They're being served by the over-powdered,
rose-beautiful, yakking waitress. Now the wasp
decides to bully them. Who reckons a rose
is a rose is a rose? Not always, it ain't.
As for me, when I talk to myself,
I do not know whom I'm addressing.

The wasp flies to the windowpane, to its prison.
So human! The door opens to the greater noise
of traffic. Enter two youthful lovers,
enter the world. Inexhaustible
the possibilities of what happens next.

Cats

One Saturday afternoon in Istanbul
on waste ground fit for a parking lot
not far from the Galata Bridge,
the hullabaloo of two cats copulating.

We observed a man built like a poster-hero,
one savage arm raised, a stone in his fist.

Cats in England are private creatures.
They fuck in private as Englishmen do.

Different country. Different cats.

Yet they make an inhuman noise
just as the English do.

I uttered an unarmoured, 'Leave 'em alone.'
The poster-hero ignored me
as much as the busy cats ignored him.
He stooped, he weighed another stone.

On behalf of the British Council (who had hired me)
and all animal lovers
(these two cats were animal lovers!)
not to mention D. H. Lawrence
and the sanctity of love-making
(the subject of my future lecture)
I asked my translator to translate.

After a protein-rich Turkish dialogue
the muscular No of a man
continued to shower stones on the cats
and the cats continued their joyous coupling.

'He's stoning them,' explained my translator,
'because he says they're both male cats.'

Grimly I stared at the grim poster-hero and
the more I stared the more he grew
more muscular. I turned away without valour
and soon, as if by appointment,
we encountered an unjudging beggar.
Gratefully, I dropped a few coins in his cap.

Song of the Crow

'From faraway, I,
messenger of malign news,
flew under reversing clouds
fast as my shadow
on the waters below.
Never resting. Another 100 miles,
then again another 100 miles,
me and my little black shadow,
simply to find your town,
your street, your home,
your face at the window.'

So it sang its gride song
and I heard it
beyond the glass,
shabby, hopping on the snow,
this way, that way,
to fall silent at last,

to look about furtively,
that way, *this* way,
before marking with vicious beak
a cross in the snow.

Then it stretched its black wings wide.

(After Primo Levi)

Wagner

After the sick adventure and insolence
of steep soaring notes, heaven-lit,
the romantic convulsive fall and
fall to nuances of German black.

The suited orchestra inhabit the pit –
like the dead must be hidden.
Cthonic music must come back as if
bidden from the deeps of the earth.

Wagner, is this your dream or Wotan's?
An organ dismembered, a sexual shout,
scream and burn – climax of a candle-flame
blown out, more a woman's than a man's.

Genius with the soul of a vulture
your overgrown music is good for heroes,
for cheap Hollywood; yet there's something else,
something taciturn, almost remembered.

Outside the Hall even your statue, moon-blown,
stone-deaf, smells of the urn; and ghosts soaped
in moonlight weep. The streets of Germany
are clean, like the hands of Lady Macbeth.

And does your stern distinguished statue keep
vigil for another Fuhrer's return?
Some statues never awaken,
some never seem to sleep.

Rilke's Confession

Whoever weeps somewhere in the night
without comfort
mimics me

Whoever laughs somewhere in the night
without cause
frightens me

Whoever wanders somewhere in the night
without purpose
counsels me

Whoever screams somewhere in the night
without mercy
bruises me

Whoever makes love somewhere in the night
without love
rebukes me

Whoever dies somewhere in the night
with no-one by
precedes me

Side Effects

Ghosts released from Time walked into the world of light –
a drug's mistake, this glimpse of the other world.
I was close to Eternity the other night.

I observed the evolution of angels into birds
and Lilith screaming, her umbilical cord tied to earth.
I won't repeat the demonic squalor of her words.

The shock of the Old! Permanent her fate, her frailty.
Her scream changed into an ambulance's siren
when they hurried me back in time to Casualty.

Now home from Zohar's frantic country where Death dies
I celebrate the Big Bang, strange thing born of a mistake,
beautiful side-effect, magic of sundown and sunrise,

this Earth unbalanced and spinning among the stars.

A Political Prisoner

*Franco could have freed Miguel Hernandez from prison. How could a
shepherd boy used to living in the open air live seven years in prison.
He got TB. His execution was carried out by Tuberculosis.* Neruda

I

The noise of many knuckles on metal,
we do not hear it.
There is lightning when we are asleep
and thunder that does not speak;
there are guitars without strings
and nightingales with tongues of glass.

Yet even if we imagine it,
the metal sound of bolts shut to,
then feet stamping down echoing corridors,

what can we do who stroll on easy grass,
who smile back at the gracious and the
goodlooking?

Righteous the rhetoric of indignation,
but protesting poems, like the plaster angels,
are impotent. They commit no crimes,
they pass no laws; they grant amnesty
only to those who, in safety, write them.

2

Shepherd from the village, Orihuela,
who, whistling, could mimic different birds,
who, by day, would count the cabra and
by night, from the hills, the straying stars,
you opened your eyelids noiselessly,
found you were sitting, hunched in a cell.
You howled, hurled a bucket at the bars.

Far from the villanelle of nightingales
or the sexual moan in the throat of doves,
they handed you a bible, remarked slyly,
'Poet, feel at home.' Then Hell's Time
seemed to strike its palindrome note
and you knew you would perish in that cell.
'Flesh falls off gradually,
bones collapse suddenly,' you wrote.

Boxed in a dark, lone prisoners still rot
everywhere in the world. Some tortured, some not,

some emaciated like you coughing out
bacilli and blood in dawn's delirium
while, near and remote, indifferent birds
sweetly sing or corvine croak.

They threw you a lemon. 'It was sour,' you wrote.

1966, 2014

Poet in the Classroom

First draw an oblong on an unlined page,
the shape of the page. Now what do you see?

No, Peter, no. Not an upright coffin.
Hardly, it's much too wide for that. Mmm?

A magician's box, uh huh. Suppose so.
From which the blonde lady has disappeared

no doubt. What do you think, Melanie? Yes,
a window. Right. What do you see through it?

Snowfields? Acres of snowfields on and on?
Quiet, Mary. It's Melanie's window.

What? A frosted window? C'mon, hardly.
Someone in a bath behind it, perhaps.

Henry, what do you see? Yes, what you've drawn.
I see sir . . . an oblong on a blank page.

Why are you laughing, Peter? What's that, Paul?
Mmm. A cage without bars. The bird has flown.

From the next classroom I heard children sing,
'The minstrel boy to the war is gone . . .'

and I thought of the real world and its ills
and the uselessness of doodling oblongs,

Then of my true vocation. And do I
do little more than doodle oblongs?

What canst thou do? Thou art a dreaming thing.

Later, though, I cycled home almost happy.

Peace in Our Time

When they vow
a subtle perfume,
tactful dilutions
of musk, civet, ambergris,

expect a computer error:
a veritable gasworks.
Dry in the vibrating air
plain H_2S.

When they promise
a hundredpiece orchestra,
Brahms, Berlioz, Mahler –
Three Blind Mice on a comb.

When a King's golden crown,
a party paper hat:
when a Queen's diamond,
a globule of glass.

When a champagne night
at the Ritz
with stunning Delilah,
a haircut.

When 100 virgins in heaven
none quite as old
as Methuselah . . .
Pardon?

Consider the double suicide pact
of Mr and Mrs Maltby.
As agreed, he shot her first,
then was unable.

Gently he undressed her,
as he had in life:
he propped her up
naked in the bath.

Night after night
brought lit candles
into that bathroom
where he quietly dined:

faithfully choosing
her favourite dishes –
fish mainly, turbot, trout,
kindly removing the bones.

First World War Hero

Often away on business though no-one
seemed to know what Uncle's business was.
He'd return from Timbuktu, North Pole or Mars,
cigar-smoking, proud of his new bought Bentley.

Not always a Bentley. Sometimes a cavalier Rolls
or some other post-war car made in Heaven.
'Sam juggles cars like he juggles lemons,'
Dad grumbled. We owned an Austin 7.

Once, with three lemons, Uncle entranced me.
He danced over watchful one-eyed daisies
juggling a choreograph of lemons. Funny, freckled
red-haired Uncle. Such beauty of balance!

He could do it with whisky wizardry,
kneeling on the floor, singing a Fred Astaire song
but mother disapproved of war-hero Sam.
'Generous with other people's money. Scab. Cheat.'

'Not a cheat,' Dad frowned. 'A juggler, yes,
a meshugana charmer and chancer, yes. Always
was, always will be till his name's on the slab
he'll throw up Sour till it comes down Sweet.'

No exemplar, but misled, I was in awe of Sam.
They said at Ypres he had killed ten Huns.
Asked about his medals he fled into silence,
then winked, 'They gave me them for juggling lemons.'

That was whisky-glib years ago. Now no more
cars, leaping lemons. At Sam's funeral, drama:
Aunt numb and an unknown woman weeping
comforted by a freckled, red-haired son.

In the trance of Belief there are spaced-out gurus,
wild messiahs, and can-do men like Sam,
tight-rope stars, in god-fearless equipoise,
they speak to a child and to the child in man.

The End of the Affair

(Harriet's)

Am I, Harriet, this April an April Fool?
I'll not accept your handshake offer:
'Friendship' – though what persists of love
lies chilled in the past, illusory,
like the voyaging far light of a star.

I'm not benign like Shelley's Harriet, no,
though pregnant as she was and as wretched.
I'll not saccharine a suicide-note
'Dear one, God bless and watch over you,'
then grow hideous in the Serpentine.

Or be helpless like pill-taking Sylvia
for whom the sloven dog Cerberus barked
(those oneiric poems SOS's)
before full-stopping the febrile heart
with her head, eyes open, in the oven.

Yet once, like her, I hoped for a hundred
piece orchestra, and Beethoven and Berlioz,
not a thin pop-tune on a tin whistle;
a happy-ever-after golden crown,
not a dunce's paper hat, twee and tatty.

Don't you see? It's the blood-filled poetry
of love's adult passion I long for still,
its wild rhyming and its cadences
– this the dismayed heart of it –
not the attenuated prose of friendship,

your mild pity, God rot your smiling teeth,
the pretty blossom's looted, betrayed,
the wind and the cold of it – April's
practical joke: the trees' confetti
wet and finished in the gutters.

Angels in the National Gallery

Each single angel is terrible
R.M. Rilke

Not these, hardly these, not even Piero's
smoothy-faced St Michael, despite big sword
in one hand, nasty snake's head in other;
certainly not angel Gabriel, mild,
bored with his pose of kneeling for Fra Lippi;

all said and done, a mere silly, pre-pubertal boy
with a simpering look of 'Gee, you're pregnant!',
overdressed Sunday-best peacock's wings
that would not lift him higher than a tree.
And those other angels (God permitting)
who granted impure painters with pure ability

a sitting – how unhappy they appear,
androgynous holy ones with male names
(designated long legends ago, of course, by men)
so tame, surely, that if you cried hosannas,

clapped hands loudly, they'd disappear slowly
back to where they belong, vast Invisibility.

Rilke, only those never portrayed in paintings,
like reprobate angels Emim and Azabel,
are terrible. They dwell deep in mirrors,
visible if self is stared at too long,
and would bring our burdened, balanced world
to a blazing fall as they, in smoke, once fell.

Alzheimer's

8 jars of nothing
And 1 jar of barley sugar
 2 jars of acid drops
 3 jars of chocolate drops
 4 jars of liquorice allsorts
 5 jars of mintoes
 6 jars of humbugs
 7 jars of bulls' eyes.

An old-age adagio, cello-sad.
Suspicions, accusations,
whisperings of the profane,
the enthronement of doubt.
Then a turning back

to the bleak mechanism.
Aphasia, agnosia,
a blank 75" record, black
like the far farmhouse
that merges with
night-surrounding fields
when the electric
in the high bedroom
at last goes out

And 7 jars of bulls' eyes
    6 jars of humbugs
    5 jars of mintoes
    4 jars of liquorice allsorts
    3 jars of

Solace

On her deathbed my spunky mother
wishing to be left alone, not helped,
cursed me. My hand, mid-air, still as stone.
Her sudden gritty voice jarring and unjust,
a snarling stranger's voice, sister of one
who knew the 32 curses of Leviticus.
The Dukes of Edom would have been amazed,
the Mighty of Moab would have been undone.

That night each man cursed became my brother.

Today I read how Rabbi Simeon's son
had been vilely cursed: *May your permanent
home be ruined, may your temporary
abodes be built up.* 'These are blessings not
curses,' Simeon interpreted, cocksure.
'You are wished Long Life so that your own
    plot
in the family cemetery be ruined,
and the houses wherein you live endure.'

1989, 2014

My Little Red Flower

Now summer has come to my garden
and a thing of phenogamous beauty has come
half hidden below the shadow darkness of a bush.

Almost luminous, it peeps from behind a leaf
with a daring redness that commands Stop!
Admire me.

Not a proud Lawrentian geranium,
not an opium-tranced poppy or luscious rose
of improvident scent.
What?

To know its name I buy a colour-plated
encyclopedia of flowers.
Not listed there.

This sun-sauced morning I open the front door
to two sombre strangers.
They carry night-black, official-looking books
and religious tracts.
Do you know the end of the world is nigh?

I reply Yes and they are manifestly disappointed.
When I confess I keep a packed suitcase
ready upstairs,
they retreat with Olympic pace.

Goodbye you spies of Thanatos
but I recall once more, fact and paradox,
that without the life-giving warmth of the sun
vultures do not fly.

Afterwards, I happen to glance at my nameless
little red flower.
It seems even more beautiful than before.

Soap Bubbles

(For Dylan's 100th Birthday)

You liked your Aunt's madeira-cake front room
over-furnished with a stuffed fox (after its last death)
about to spit, with scripture-texted walls
and a staring clock muttering an accusing tick.

There, once, the small Dylan you were
stood clapping hands while soap bubbles floated,
strayed, lingered in coloured transparencies
of cathedral windows. 'Dilly, Dilly,' your Aunt teased,
'Jump. Catch them.'

It was the big god's injurious conjuring trick.
First you see them, pretty pretty, then you don't.

What child wouldn't want one becalmed bubble
not to burst, a door to open for its triumphant exit,
to drift over a cwmdonkin-like park
where, amazed, summerhouse Red Indians shout
'Pax,' and the grieving lovers and hunchbacks laugh?

But nothing will be unless something was.
The bubbles on fire exploded without a sound,
vanished on a Welsh Dresser tall as a small giraffe,
on chairs bleak-brown as owls, on scolding
religious walls or, damned, were swallowed down
by the once shot, woken-up, sly stuffed fox.

Fade. Cut.
Vultures roost in the parks of Arcady
and the cadaver is in the child.

Now Jubal's favoured poet who searched
for the gate marked BACK, is 100 years old
and Dilly Dilly Dylan (come and be killed),
unlike Willie Willie Wee, is dead dead dead.

Oh my dead dear, all's vanished.

Who heard the little thud of a book being shut?

Birthday Card for Fleur

Always, Fleur, we two nudge each other
in perdurable friendship on the top shelves
of Waterstones. Books almost out of reach
as we are to our own unfathomable selves.

Today, in the treasure of solitude,
(there is a shaking bombsite world elsewhere)
I read your spare poetry with rare pleasure
(you know the secrets of lucidity)
and recall the Sixties, the easy years
when we met and who we thought we were.

Bliss was it then, each sundown, to be young.
(At 80 to be asleep at dawn is very heaven!)
But do I see the dazzle of 80 candles?
It cannot be. I look at you. Something is amiss.

Dear Fleur, I send you this awkward birthdaycard,
the precious balm of truthful flattery,
and a companionable handblown kiss.

Two for Lynne

1

First Meeting

Sweet youthful widow
of such a wistful countenance
do we need second sight
to know love at first sight?

No-one gabbled on and on about chance
and fate and the wheeling stars.

Simply when you came near me
you trembled as aspen leaves do
and I, like Simon Magus,
thought I would levitate.

2

Like

an English summer's day?
Child at the windowpane, cherub

driving all the family mad
with what shall I do mam?
When will it stop raining, mam?
till cherub's big brother shouts shut-up
and the little lunatic weeps
and outside the sky's a remorseless grey
and the darling buds of May, wet, odourless.

I think, Not like.

And a No to Burns's self-admiring
red red rose – too June insolent, too
overblown, too wantonly perfumed;
rather I would compare thee
to those shyest of flowers
that must be held so close
before their scent is known.

Ask the Moon

I

Wakeful past 3 a.m.
near the frontiers of Nothing
it's easy, so easy
to imagine (like William Blake)
an archaic angel standing askew

in a cone of light
not of this world;

easy at this cheating hour
to believe an angel cometh
to touch babies' skulls,
their fontanelles,
deleting the long memory
of generations –
the genesis of déja vu;

easy to conceive angel-light
bright as that sudden
ordinary window
I saw at midnight
across the road
before the drawing of a blind.

2

Once another presence
also nocturnal, oneiric,
secretive, in disguise,
waiting behind
an opening Seder door.

'No,' says the child, 'Gone.'
Framed in that black oblong
nobody.

(A shadow flees
when a light is shone.)

Was childhood real?
Did a stallion attempt
to mount a mare
painted by Apelles, as they said?
Did Greek workmen really believe
that the statue to be exiled
would sob when carried to
Lord Elgin's ship? As they said.

The deceived don't know they're deceived.
When prying Apion, with eerie conch,
summoned Homer's spirit
to ask where he was born
whose bloody head,
for one moment only,
seemed to appear above the parapet?

Ask the moon.
The mystery named
is not the mystery caged.

Even a night-scene
may be an illusion, a fake,
like an afternoon harbour
viewed through sunglasses,
the light forged over
a moon-tormented sea.

3

I was visited once, once only, elsewhere,
near a lake, near an oak,
near a weeping willow tree and thorn
one summertime, out of time, in England,
during the cosmic love-making hour
when day and night shyly intermingle,

when day entranced does not know
what or when and night, ecstatic,
is not itself entirely
till the late coming of the stars.

But now it's 4 a.m. already
and like a snow-flake's touch
shiver-cold and quiet.

     Did someone cry out?
I heard someone cry out.
    No-one cried out.

I woke up dreaming I
    was wide-awake.

Gone

Always I wanted to hear the heartbeat
of words and summoned you, oneiric one.
I changed your feathers to purple and to white.

So what did you, ventriloquist bird, say
besides, It's closing time, old dear?
You only spoke when compelled –

as when the long whistle blew on happiness
or when sunlight was such a dazzle
you flew into it, thinking you could sing.

Wide awake or half asleep you liked to be
deceptive, yet never babblative enough
to employ the bald serious scholars.

Odd that I imagined you could wear
and blend purple feathers with the white
to abate the panic of a blank page.

When I fed you with my two lives you took
your fill of both and soliloquised.
Always your style was in the error

and the Beatrice I loved praised your endeavour
to grasp at what cannot be grasped
in the pursuance of the incomplete

Sometimes, dionysiac, you choired loudly,
(the drama of an exclamation mark!)
and sometimes you word-whispered sedately.

Now I'm tired and you nest elsewhere.
Bird, your cage is empty. You cannot come back.
Eros is disarmed and Thanatos is here.

So long, proud parrot! Until the last
you beat your wings against the mirror-world,
your voice a contrast of the harsh and sweet.

Valediction

In this exile people call old age
I lived between nostalgia and rage.
This is the land of fools and fear.
Thanks be. I was lucky to be here.